30 DAYS

TO

UNDERSTANDING

THE BIBLE

UNLOCK THE SCRIPTURES IN 15 MINUTES A DAY

STUDY GUIDE | SIX LESSONS

MAX ANDERS

THOMAS NELSON
Since 1798

CONTENTS

HOW TO USE THIS STUDY GUIDE

Let's make a bargain. If you will give me fifteen minutes a day for the next six weeks, I will give you an understanding of the Bible. In the course of this study, you will learn the story of the entire Bible . . . the major characters, major events, major points of geography, and major doctrines. You will be able to put these people and facts together in their proper chronological order and trace the geographic movement as you think your way through the entire Bible.

What is more, you will do this with a group of people like yourself who also want to gain a greater understanding of the story, history, geography, and teachings of the Bible. With this in mind, we have developed this study to be experienced in a group setting such as a Bible study, Sunday school class, or any small group gathering. Each session begins with a welcome section and two questions to get you and your group thinking about the topic. You will then watch a video featuring Max Anders and engage in some small-group discussion.

During the week, you will maximize the impact of this course by completing five daily personal studies, each of which has been designed to take fifteen minutes to complete. You will also be encouraged at the end of the first session to select one person from the group to serve as your partner throughout the course. You will check in with this person during the week to reflect on what you have learned and share your insights together.

All of the small-group members should have their own copy of this study guide. Each member is also encouraged to have a copy of the *30 Days to Understanding the Bible* book, as reading it alongside the curriculum will provide deeper insights and will make the journey more meaningful. (See the "For Next Week" section at the end of each between-studies section for the chapters in the book that correspond to the material you and your group are discussing.)

To get the most out of your group experience, keep the following points in mind. First, the real growth in this study will happen during your small-group time. This is where you will process the content of the teaching for the week, ask questions, and learn from others as you hear what God is doing in their lives. For this reason, it is important for you to be fully committed to the group and attend each session so you can build trust and rapport with the other members. If you choose to only go through the motions, or if you refrain from participating, there is a lesser chance you will find what you're looking for during this study.

Second, remember that the goal of your small group is to serve as a place where people can share, learn about God, and also build intimacy and friendship. For this reason, seek to make your group a safe place. This means being honest about your thoughts and feelings and listening carefully to everyone else's opinion. (If you are a group leader, there are additional instructions and resources in the back of the book for leading a productive discussion group.)

Third, resist the temptation to fix a problem people in the group might be having or to correct their theology, as that is not the purpose of your small-group time. Also, keep everything your group shares confidential. This will foster a rewarding sense of community in your group and create a place where people can heal, be challenged, and grow spiritually.

The Bible is an enormous book covering much information and many subjects. It is simply not possible to learn everything about it in six weeks. But you can gain a beginning knowledge—and overview—that you can use to build a more complete understanding in the years ahead. Over the course of this study, you can gain a foundational grasp of the most important book ever written. So, let's get started!

— Max Anders

AN OVERVIEW OF THE BIBLE

If you want to learn architecture, you must first learn how buildings
are put together. If you want to learn sailing, you must first learn
how ships are put together. And if you want to understand the Bible,
you must first learn how the Bible is put together.

MAX ANDERS

9/14/2020

WELCOME

Welcome to *30 Days to Understanding the Bible*! This is the first step on a journey that can revolutionize your understanding not only of Scripture, but also yourself and the world around you. The Bible is the bestselling, most-loved, and most-impactful book ever written. Actually, the Bible isn't a single book—it is a collection of sixty-six books written by more than forty individuals over a period of more than 2,000 years. It's an enormous volume that contains a huge amount of information on a wide range of topics—including history, poetry, prophecy, geography, instructions, epistles, commandments, promises, and more.

For these reasons, the Bible can often seem intimidating . . . and even overwhelming. Maybe you have tried to learn about the Bible in the past and found it difficult to understand. Maybe you have been reading the Bible for years, yet you still lack confidence when it comes to expressing what it is and what it says. Or, maybe this is the first time you have opened its pages.

Regardless of your level of experience, what you will encounter with your group over the course of the next six weeks will provide a key to unlocking what the Bible says, what it teaches, and how to apply it to your everyday life. Through the videos that accompany each session, and the daily interactions in this study guide, you will build a solid foundation for engaging and understanding the most important book ever written.

SHARE

To get started, take a few minutes to introduce yourself to anyone you do not know in the group. Then jump into the theme of this session by discussing the following questions:

- How would you describe your level of understanding of the Bible at this point in your life? Beginner? Intermediate? Advanced?

- What are you hoping you will learn about the Bible during this study?

WATCH

Play the video segment for session one. As you watch, follow along with the main points listed in the outline below and record any key thoughts or concepts that stand out to you.

I. **The Promise:** If you commit to spending fifteen minutes a day in this study for the next six weeks, you will receive an understanding of the entire Bible.

A. It possible to understand each of the major people, major places, and major events of the Bible.

   1. The problem many people have with the Bible is that they start out by studying the details without ever getting the big picture.
   2. This study will focus on the big picture first and save the details for later.

B. When gaining an understanding of the Bible as a whole, it is important to focus on the broad strokes.

   1. There are thousands of mountain peaks in Colorado, but there are only fifty-three that rise over 14,000 feet.

   2. This study will focus on the "fourteeners" of God's Word,
      which is a manageable amount of information to process.

II. **Structure:** A key to mastering the Old Testament is under-
    standing that it contains only three types of books.

   A. These three types of books are:

      1. Historical books   *history*
      2. Poetical books   *poetry*
      3. Prophetical books   *Prophecy*

   B. There are seventeen historical books in the Old Testament.

      1. Only eleven of those books are primary. The other six are
         secondary.
      2. So, if you want to get your mind around the story of the Old
         Testament, you need to read Genesis, Exodus, Numbers,
         Joshua, Judges, 1 Samuel, 2 Samuel, 1 Kings, 2 Kings,
         Ezra, and Nehemiah.
      3. These eleven books create a timeline into which you can
         fit the secondary historical books, the poetic books, and
         the prophetic books.

III. **Geography:** In addition to understanding the structure of the
     Bible, it is important to also understand the broad strokes of
     biblical geography.

   A. The entire area described in the Old Testament is about the
      same size as the state of Texas.
   B. Israel, the promised land for God's people in the Old Testa-
      ment, is roughly the same size as New Hampshire.

OLD TESTAMENT BOOKS

Primary:	Job	Isaiah
Genesis	Psalms	Jeremiah
Exodus	Proverbs	Lamentations
Numbers	Ecclesiastes	Ezekiel
Joshua	Song of Solomon	Daniel
Judges		Hosea
1 Samuel		Joel
2 Samuel		Amos
1 Kings		Obadiah
2 Kings		Jonah
Ezra		Micah
Nehemiah		Nahum
		Habakkuk
Secondary:		Zephaniah
Leviticus		Haggai
Deuteronomy		Zechariah
Ruth		Malachi
1 Chronicles		
2 Chronicles		
Esther		

the story of the OT

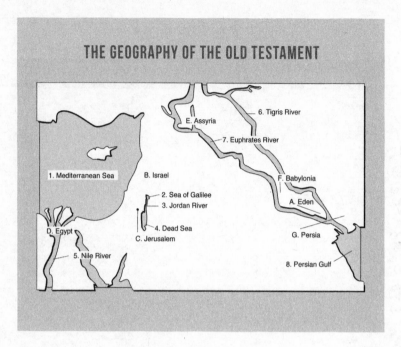

IV. **History:** The Bible's historical books cover twelve eras of the biblical story.

    A. In the Old Testament:

        1. **Creation Era:** the creation of the world and humankind, and early events. *Creation, Fall, Flood, Tower of Babel*

        2. **Patriarch Era:** the birth of the Hebrew people through a family of patriarchs, covered a period of 200 years.

        3. **Exodus Era:** the exodus of the Hebrew people as they are delivered out of 400 years of slavery in Egypt to return to their Promised Land.

        4. **Conquest Era:** the conquest of the Promised Land by the Hebrew people after their exodus from Egypt.

5. **Judges Era:** a period of 400 years during which Israel was governed by rulers known as judges.
6. **Kingdom Era:** an additional period of 400 years during which Israel was a full-fledged nation ruled by a monarchy.
7. **Exile Era:** a period of seventy years during which the Jewish people were in exile, having been conquered by foreign powers.
8. **Return Era:** the return of the exiled Jewish people to Jerusalem to rebuild the city and the temple.
9. **Silence Era** a final period of 400 years between the close of the Old Testament and the opening of the New Testament.

B. In the New Testament:

1. **Gospel Era:** the life of Jesus of Nazareth as told in the Gospels.
2. **Church Era:** the formation of the Christian church.
3. **Missions Era:** the expansion of the church into the Roman Empire through missions.

V. **Creation Era:** The story of creation, the fall, the flood, and the tower of Babel.

A. **Creation:** God created everything in the universe out of nothing.
B. **Fall:** Adam and Eve were deceived by Satan and chose to rebel against God, which ushered sin into the world.
C. **Flood:** God performed a radical surgery on the world's population, removing the cancer of evil through a worldwide flood.

THE BIBLICAL ERAS			
ERA	FIGURE	LOCATION	REFERENCE
Creation	Adam	Eden	Genesis 1–11
Patriarch	Abraham	Canaan	Genesis 12–50
Exodus	Moses	Egypt	Exodus–Deuteronomy
Conquest	Joshua	Canaan	Joshua
Judges	Samson	Canaan	Judges–Ruth
Kingdom	David	Israel	1 Samuel–2 Chronicles
Exile	Daniel	Babylonia	Ezekiel–Daniel
Return	Ezra	Jerusalem	Ezra–Esther
Silence	Pharisees	Jerusalem	–
Gospel	Jesus	Israel	Matthew–John
Church	Peter	Jerusalem	Acts 1–12
Missions	Paul	Roman Empire	Acts 13–28

    D. **Tower of Babel:** Humanity again rejected God's command to spread out, inhabit and civilize the earth, instead attempting to establish a single civilization.

VI. **Review**

    A. The structure of the Old Testament includes historical books, poetical books, and prophetical books.

    B. Knowing the geography the Bible enables its history and its story to come alive.

    C. The Creation describes the earliest events in God's Word, including the creation the world, the Fall, the Flood, and the Tower of Babel.

DISCUSS

After watching the video, use the following questions to unpack what you learned as a group.

1. What did you find most interesting about the teaching in this session? What is your greatest takeaway from what was covered?

    _____

    _____

    _____

    _____

    _____

2. What questions do you have after watching the video?

    _____

    _____

    _____

    _____

    _____

3. In your mind, why is it helpful to understand the structure of the Bible and the types of material that it contains?

    _____

    _____

    _____

    _____

    _____

    _____

    _____

4. How does it influence your understanding of the Bible to learn that most of the action takes place within an area that is only the size of Texas?

_____

_____

_____

_____

_____

5. In the teaching, you were introduced to the concept of "four-teeners" in the Bible, which means focusing on just those people and ideas that are most critical to understanding the broad strokes of the Bible. What are some "fourteeners" from the Creation Era of the biblical timeline?

_____

_____

_____

_____

_____

_____

6. The Fall is the low point of the Creation Era. How would you explain, in your own words, why Adam and Eve sinned?

_____

_____

_____

_____

_____

_____

APPLY

Understanding the Bible is a critical step for anyone who seeks to follow God—but it is never the final step. Instead, understanding what God's Word says should always lead you to apply those truths in your life. In other words, knowledge should always lead to obedience. For this reason, each section of this study will include both material to learn and recommendations for putting what you have learned into practice.

Furthermore, following the truth of the Bible is not only something you do as an individual, but also something you do in community with other Christians. For that reason, the application sections in this study will encourage you to connect with a partner (or a small group of fellow participants) as you put what you learn into practice.

To get started, choose a partner or partners (or if your group is smaller, you may choose to do this as a group) who will join with you in seeking to grow over the next six weeks of this study. As you close this session, take a moment to discuss your thoughts. What are you feeling as you get started? What was something that stood out to you in this first lesson? What are you hoping to learn or experience as a result of going through this study?

BETWEEN-SESSIONS STUDY

I f you have not already started reading *30 Days to Understanding the Bible*, now is a great time to begin. This week, you may want to read the introduction and chapters 1–4 in the book before engaging in the following between-sessions activities. Be sure to read the reflection questions after each activity and make a few notes in your guide about the experience. There will be a few minutes for you to share any insights you learned at the start of the next session.

DAY 1: INTRODUCTION TO THE BIBLE

What is your goal for working through this study? I have shared one of my main goals in the title of this resource: *30 Days to Understanding the Bible*. The key word is *understanding*. Understanding the Bible is not easy . . . but it can be made much easier than it often is.

As we said, it is helpful to start with the "fourteeners," and a significant "fourteener" is learning the structure of how the Bible is put together. In any endeavor—whether writing a term paper, building a house, figuring out how to play a piece of music, or anything else—you first need to have an overview of where you are going and how to put things together. The same is true of the Bible. if you want to understand it and learn where it is leading you, you need to know how it is put together.

This is our goal for the material that you will encounter during the course of the next six weeks. To get started today on this journey, we will look at the two major structural divisions of the Bible: the Old Testament and the New Testament. One note as we begin: because there's not enough time to explore specific Bible verses in the video content, we will make that a priority in these daily interactions. By the time you finish these thirty days of study, you will engage some of the most important passages in all of Scripture.

THE OLD TESTAMENT

The first thirty-nine books of the Bible make up what we call the Old Testament. As you saw in the video teaching this week, seventeen of those books are historical. If you want to understand the story of the Hebrew nation, you must read these books, for they compose a historical timeline for the nation of Israel. Five of the books in the Old Testament are poetical, which means they primarily contain poems, songs, and wise sayings. The remaining seventeen books are prophetic, which means they contain proclamations and prophecies concerning the Israelites.

The Old Testament not only instructed the Israelites in how they were to relate to God, but it also provides instruction to those of us in the New Testament. Today, we no longer sacrifice animals to maintain our fellowship with God, but we are to obey the principles that we find in the Old Testament, especially as they are reiterated in the New Testament.

Read the following verses found in the New Testament that alert us to the value of the Old Testament in our lives today:

These things happened to them [people in the Old Testament] as examples and were written down as warnings

for us, on whom the culmination of the ages has come
(1 Corinthians 10:11).

For everything that was written in the past was written
to teach us, so that through the endurance taught in
the Scriptures and the encouragement they provide we
might have hope (Romans 15:4).

A vital lesson from the Old Testament that carries across
into our day today is the importance of believing and trusting
God, and as a result, obeying Him.

How does the story of the Old Testament provide a warning for
our lives today about the importance of faith and obedience (see
1 Corinthians 10:11)?

_____

_____

_____

How does the Old Testament encourage us and give us hope today
regarding the importance of faith and obedience (see Romans 15:4)?

_____

_____

_____

_____

THE NEW TESTAMENT

The New Testament centers on the life, ministry, and impact of
Jesus Christ as a historical figure. The twenty-seven books that
make up the New Testament serve as the record of Jesus' birth,

His ministry, and the ministry of His disciples and apostles, which was carried on after He was crucified.

The New Testament begins with four historical accounts of Jesus' life (we refer to these as the Gospels: Matthew, Mark, Luke, and John) and the book of the Acts of the Apostles. The rest of the New Testament is comprised of letters—also known as epistles—which were written by leaders of the early church to provide guidance and structure for living as followers of Jesus in an often-hostile world.

Read the following verses found in the New Testament describing the coming of Christ:

> In the beginning was the Word, and the Word was with God, and the Word was God. He was with God in the beginning. Through him all things were made; without him nothing was made that has been made. In him was life, and that life was the light of all mankind. The light shines in the darkness, and the darkness has not overcome it. . . .
>
> The Word became flesh and made his dwelling among us. We have seen his glory, the glory of the one and only Son, who came from the Father, full of grace and truth (John 1:1–5, 14).

What does this passage teach us about who Jesus is?

_____

_____

_____

_____

_____

_____

What does this passage teach us about what He did before He was born as Jesus of Nazareth?

_____

_____

_____

_____

_____

REVIEW

At the end of each day, you will be asked to fill in some blanks. This is because repetition is the key to mental ownership. By being faithful to complete the review exercises, you will not only gain mastery of important information today, but you will also create a powerful foundation of knowledge that will enable multiplied learning tomorrow. (For this exercise, refer to the notes you took in the "Watch" portion of this week's group study section.)

- There are _____ books in the Old Testament and _____ books in the New Testament. There are _____ books in the entire Bible.
- The Old Testament is the story of God and the _____ people, their poets, and their prophets.
- There are three kinds of books in the Old Testament: _____ books, _____ books, and _____ books.

Answers to each of these review questions are in the back of this guide.

DAY 2: GEOGRAPHY OF THE OLD TESTAMENT

Isn't it amazing how quickly printed maps became a thing of the past? With smartphones and GPS satellites, they are rarely needed—but we will always need geography, which is the study of the physical features of our world. Why? Because, as we travel, we will always need to understand where we have come from and where we are going!

In a similar way, geography is critical for understanding the Bible. To be able to visualize geographic locations and movement causes the story of the Bible to come alive in our minds in a way that it will not otherwise. It allows us to remember, to connect dots, to grasp significance that we cannot do without it.

The person who is ignorant of geography cannot fully understand history—for the two subjects are closely linked. And because the Bible is largely history, we will be exploring a healthy dose of geography each week throughout this study.

BODIES OF WATER

Refer to the map in the group discussion section for this session. Notice there are eight key bodies of water identified: (1) the Mediterranean Sea, (2) the Sea of Galilee (actually a freshwater lake seven miles wide by fourteen miles long), (3) the Jordan River (which flows south out of the Sea of Galilee), (4) the Dead Sea (the lowest point on earth, almost 3,000 feet below sea level), (5) the Nile River (the most famous river in the world that flows through Egypt), (6) the Tigris River, (7) the Euphrates River, and (8) the Persian Gulf (which along with the Tigris and Euphrates forms the eastern boundary for the lands of the Old Testament).

Which of these bodies of water were you already familiar with? Which ones were new to you?

In your own words, why is it important to understand the geography of the nations, regions, and bodies of water described throughout the Old Testament?

_____

_____

_____

_____

LOCATIONS

There are seven key locations identified on the map: (A) the Garden of Eden (where everything began), (B) Israel (a land that lies between the Mediterranean coast and the Sea of Galilee-Jordan River-Dead Sea), (C) the city of Jerusalem, (D) Egypt (where the Israelites were enslaved), (E) Assyria (a great world power that conquered the northern kingdom of Israel), (F) Babylonia (a great world power that conquered the southern kingdom of Judah), and (G) Persia (the final historical superpower of the Old Testament eras).

Jerusalem is one of the most important locations in the entire Bible. It is the capital city of the nation of Israel in the Old Testament, and was the home of the Temple of Solomon, one of the most impressive buildings ever built. The center of worship for Israel, it was the most treasured location in all the nation. It was well-protected by an impressive wall and well-fortified. If other nations wanted to conquer the nation of Israel, they knew they had to conquer Jerusalem.

Located just off the northwestern shoulder of the Dead Sea, it is built atop Mount Zion and nestled within a larger mountain range in the central region of Israel, which made it difficult to attack in ancient days. The city was originally built and occupied by the Jebusites. King David was only able to conquer the city because of some creative thinking regarding its water shafts and ducts:

The king and his men marched to Jerusalem to attack the Jebusites, who lived there. The Jebusites said to David, "You will not get in here; even the blind and the lame can ward you off." They thought, "David cannot get in here." Nevertheless, David captured the fortress of Zion—which is the City of David.

On that day David had said, "Anyone who conquers the Jebusites will have to use the water shaft to reach those 'lame and blind' who are David's enemies." That is why they say, "The 'blind and lame' will not enter the palace."

David then took up residence in the fortress and called it the City of David. He built up the area around it, from the terraces inward. And he became more and more powerful, because the LORD God Almighty was with him (2 Samuel 5:6–10).

What do you know about Jerusalem as a city today?

_____

_____

_____

_____

What are three reasons why Jerusalem is an important city within the Bible?

_____

_____

_____

_____

_____

REVIEW

Fill in the blanks in the map from memory. (Refer to the notes you took in the "Watch" portion of this week's group study section if you need additional help.) Note that the blanks with numbers are bodies of water, while the blanks with letters are locations.

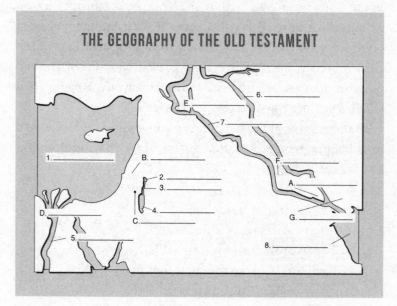

DAY 3: HISTORY IN THE BIBLE

You have likely heard the phrase, "Those who ignore history are doomed to repeat it." Well, it is also true that those who ignore the history of the Bible will never understand it. This is because the Bible is packed with historical people, places, and events.

The storyline of the Bible can be divided into twelve main eras, with a central figure and main location for each era. Nine of the eras are found in the Old Testament, and three are found in the New Testament. We will explore the nine Old Testament eras during the next two weeks, starting tomorrow with the

Creation Era. But today, we will explore what the Bible says about the importance of history by highlighting a key passage from the book of Psalms.

HISTORY IN SONG

Psalm 78, written by a man named Asaph, is a history lesson wrapped in a song. Through seventy-two verses, he expounded on the many ways God had blessed previous generations of His chosen people, the Israelites. That was the good news. The bad news was that Asaph also listed the many ways the Israelites had rebelled against God and rejected His laws.

Importantly, at the beginning of his song, Asaph offered a brief but powerful explanation on the value of paying attention to history:

> My people, hear my teaching;
>> listen to the words of my mouth.
> I will open my mouth with a parable;
>> I will utter hidden things, things from of old—
> things we have heard and known,
>> things our ancestors have told us.
> We will not hide them from their descendants;
>> **we will tell the next generation**
> **the praiseworthy deeds of the Lord,**
>> **his power, and the wonders he has done.**
> He decreed statutes for Jacob
>> and established the law in Israel,
> which he commanded our ancestors
>> to teach their children,
> so the next generation would know them,
>> even the children yet to be born,
>> and they in turn would tell their children.

> <u>Then they would put their trust in God</u>
>> <u>and would not forget his deeds</u>
>> <u>but would keep his commands.</u>
> They would not be like their ancestors—
>> a stubborn and rebellious generation,
> whose hearts were not loyal to God,
>> whose spirits were not faithful to him (Psalm 78:1–8).

Why is it important to actively teach the lessons of Bible history from generation to generation (see the bolded words in the psalm above)?

_____

_____

_____

_____

_____

_____

What result was Asaph hoping to avoid by sharing this history (see underlined words in the psalm above)?

_____

_____

_____

_____

_____

_____

REVIEW

Fill in the blanks in the following chart from memory. (Refer to the notes you took in the "Watch" portion of this week's group study section if you need additional help.)

OLD TESTAMENT ERA	REFERENCE
1.	Genesis 1–11
2.	Genesis 12–50
3.	Exodus–Deuteronomy
4.	Joshua
5.	Judges–Ruth
6.	1 Samuel–2 Chronicles
7.	Ezekiel–Daniel
8.	Ezra–Esther
9.	—
NEW TESTAMENT ERA	**REFERENCE**
1.	Matthew–John
2.	Acts 1–12
3.	Acts 13–28

DAY 4: THE CREATION AND FALL

It seems the more we learn about our universe, the more we realize how much we need to learn. From subatomic particles all the way to immeasurable galaxies, the scope of creation is immense! And that immensity says a great deal about our Creator. The Creation Era in the Bible is contained in the first eleven chapters of the Book of Genesis. Today, we will look at two main events that occur in Genesis 1–3: the creation and the fall.

THE CREATION

Perhaps more than anything else, the mystery and immensity of our universe capture our imagination and incites us to wonder about creation. God answers this question about the origin of our world in the first chapter of Genesis, where we read the following:

In the beginning God created the heavens and the earth. Now the earth was formless and empty, darkness was over the surface of the deep, and the Spirit of God was hovering over the waters.

And God said, "Let there be light," and there was light. . . . the first day. And God said, "Let there be a vault between the waters to separate water from water." . . . the second day. And God said, "Let the water under the sky be gathered to one place, and let dry ground appear." . . . Then God said, "Let the land produce vegetation: seed-bearing plants and trees on the land that bear fruit with seed in it, according to their various kinds." . . . the third day.

And God said, "Let there be lights in the vault of the sky to separate the day from the night . . . . the fourth day. And God said, "Let the water teem with living creatures, and let birds fly above the earth across the vault of the sky." . . . the fifth day. And God said, "Let the land produce living creatures according to their kinds: the livestock, the creatures that move along the ground, and the wild animals, each according to its kind." . . .

Then God said, "Let us make mankind in our image, in our likeness, so that they may rule over the fish in the sea and the birds in the sky, over the livestock and all the wild animals, and over all the creatures that move along the ground." So God created mankind in his own image, in the image of God he created them; male and female he created them. . . . the sixth day (Genesis 1:1–3, 5–6, 8–9, 11, 13–14, 19–20, 23–24, 26–27, 31).

How does the author of this passage describe the process in which God created the heavens, the earth, the creatures on the planet, and human beings?

_____

_____

_____

_____

_____

What is different about the way that God created humans from the rest of creation?

_____

_____

_____

_____

_____

THE FALL

The event known as "the Fall" happened in a single moment. Satan, appearing in the form of a serpent, lured Adam and Eve into rebelling against God and violating the one prohibition He had given them: not to eat from the tree of the knowledge of good and evil. The consequences of that moment have affected all of humanity since. Adam and Eve were driven out of Eden, and a curse fell on all creation when sin entered the world. All of the pain, evil, and suffering that humanity has endured can be traced back to this incredibly significant choice:

> Now the serpent was more crafty than any of the wild animals the LORD God had made. He said to the woman, "Did God really say, 'You must not eat from any tree in the garden'?"

The woman said to the serpent, "We may eat fruit from the trees in the garden, but God did say, 'You must not eat fruit from the tree that is in the middle of the garden, and you must not touch it, or you will die.'"

"You will not certainly die," the serpent said to the woman. "For God knows that when you eat from it your eyes will be opened, and you will be like God, knowing good and evil."

When the woman saw that the fruit of the tree was good for food and pleasing to the eye, and also desirable for gaining wisdom, she took some and ate it. She also gave some to her husband, who was with her, and he ate it. Then the eyes of both of them were opened, and they realized they were naked; so they sewed fig leaves together and made coverings for themselves (Genesis 3:1–7).

Where do you currently see evidence of the curse of sin in our world? In your own life?

_____

_____

_____

_____

_____

What are some ways humanity is still attempting to "be like God"?

_____

_____

_____

_____

REVIEW

Fill in the timeline for these events that you have learned in the Creation Era. (Refer to the passages in the "reference" column if you need additional help.)

TIMELINE	WHAT GOD CREATED/ WHAT OCCURRED	REFERENCE
Day 1 of Creation		Genesis 1:1–3
Day 2 of Creation		Genesis 1:6–8
Day 3 of Creation		Genesis 1:9–13
Day 4 of Creation		Genesis 1:14–19
Day 5 of Creation		Genesis 1:20–23
Day 6 of Creation		Genesis 1:24–31
After Creation		Genesis 3:1–24

DAY 5: THE FLOOD AND THE TOWER

Over the next several hundred years, as humans multiplied in numbers, so did their tendency to sin. Ultimately, the time came when God could only find eight people in the entire world who were willing to live in a righteous relationship with Him. The consequences that result are covered in Genesis 4–11: the flood and the Tower of Babel.

THE FLOOD

In judgment for humanity's sin, God determined to wipe out all of the evil and corrupt members of the human race and begin again with the eight righteous individuals that He had found— Noah, his wife, his three sons, and their wives. He did this by sending a flood:

> Now the earth was corrupt in God's sight and was full of violence. God saw how corrupt the earth had become, for all the people on earth had corrupted their ways. So God said to Noah, "I am going to put an end to all peo-ple, for the earth is filled with violence because of them. I am surely going to destroy both them and the earth. So make yourself an arc of cypress wood; make rooms in it and coat it with pitch inside and out. This is how you are to build it: The ark is to be three hundred cubits long, fifty cubits wide and thirty cubits high. Make a roof for it, leaving below the roof an opening one cu-bit high all around. Put a door in the side of the ark and make lower, middle and upper decks. I am going to bring floodwaters on the earth to destroy all life under the heavens, every creature that has the breath of life in it. Everything on earth will perish. But I will establish my covenant with you, and you will enter the ark—you and your sons and your wife and your sons' wives with you. You are to bring into the ark two of all living crea-tures, male and female, to keep them alive with you. Two of every kind of bird, of every kind of animal and of

every kind of creature that moves along the ground will come to you to be kept alive. You are to take every kind of food that is to be eaten and store it away as food for you and for them."

Noah did everything just as God commanded him (Genesis 6:11–22).

What are the reasons that God gave for choosing to destroy humanity?

_____

_____

_____

_____

_____

What promise did God make to Noah and his family?

_____

_____

_____

_____

THE TOWER OF BABEL

God's post-flood mandate was for humans to spread out, populate, and subdue the earth. However, in disobedience to that command, humans stayed in one place and began to build a monument to their own greatness. We read in Genesis what happened as a result:

Now the whole world had one language and a common speech. As people moved eastward, they found a plain in Shinar and settled there.

They said to each other, "Come, let's make bricks and bake them thoroughly." They used brick instead of stone, and tar for mortar. Then they said, "Come, let us build ourselves a city, with a tower that reaches to the heavens, so that we may make a name for ourselves; otherwise we will be scattered over the face of the whole earth."

But the LORD came down to see the city and the tower the people were building. The LORD said, "If, as one people speaking the same language they have begun to do this, then nothing they plan to do will be impossible for them. Come, let us go down and confuse their language so they will not understand each other."

So the LORD scattered them from there over all the earth, and they stopped building the city. That is why it was called Babel—because there the LORD confused the language of the whole world. From there the LORD scattered them over the face of the whole earth (Genesis 11:1–9).

What were the reasons the people gave for wanting to build the tower?

_____

_____

_____

_____

What were God's purposes in confusing their languages?

_____

_____

_____

_____

REVIEW

Write the correct number in the blank from the options on the right. (Refer to the notes you took in the "Watch" portion of this week's group study section if you need additional help.)

EVENT		DESCRIPTION
Creation:		1. Judgment for sin (Genesis 6:13)
Fall:		2. Beginning of the nations (Genesis 11:8–9)
Flood:		3. Sin entered the world (Genesis 3:6–7)
Tower:		4. Humans made in God's image (Genesis 1:26)

Fill in the blanks from memory:

ERA	SUMMARY
Creation:	Adam is created by God, but he _____. This is known as "the _____." This destroys God's original _____ for humans.

APPLY

Check in with your partner each week to review and discuss what you studied. Use the following questions to help determine those goals and cement the main concepts in your minds.

- **Introduction:** Discuss what you hope to learn during the course of this study. Also discuss in what areas you would like to grow spiritually.

- **Geography:** Look up some news articles to see what has been happening in Jerusalem recently. When you meet this week, pray, in the words of Psalm 122:6, for the "peace of Jerusalem"—asking that God would protect the city and keep its citizens from harm.

- **History:** Discuss some of the lessons that you have learned from personal past mistakes—especially those moments when you turned away from God. Discuss how reflecting on those mistakes might keep you from future mistakes.

- **Creation and the Fall:** Adam and Eve's choice to rebel against God was rooted in the belief that, in order to be truly happy, they needed something more than God was giving to them. Discuss where you might be tempted to go outside the will of God to get something that you (mistakenly) believe you need in order to be truly happy.

- **The Flood and the Tower:** Discuss the importance of obeying God's instructions—even if they might not make sense to you.

FOR NEXT WEEK

Use the space below to write any insights or questions from your personal study that you want to discuss at the next group meeting. In preparation for next week, review chapters 5–9 in *30 Days to Understanding the Bible*.

THE EARLY HISTORY OF ISRAEL

PATRIARCH — KINGDOM ERAS

By nature, humans desire something they cannot have:
total freedom. The people of Israel wanted total freedom.
They wanted the freedom to ignore the directives that God
had given. As a result, the early history of Israel tended to be a
turbulent time, with many ups and downs.

MAX ANDERS

WELCOME

Welcome to the second group session for *30 Days to Understanding the Bible*. If there is one thing that I have learned from decades as a teacher—and especially as a teacher of the Bible—it is that repetition is a key tool for understanding something new. As I say all the time, repetition is the key to mental ownership. So let's take a few moments as we begin to review the ground you have covered so far on this journey toward understanding God's Word.

As we discussed in the previous session, understanding the structure of the Bible provides a key to unlocking its mysteries. The Bible contains sixty-six books in total, but they are not all the same types of books. First, the Bible is divided into the Old and New Testaments, with Jesus Christ as the dividing point between them. Second, when we look specifically at the Old Testament, we find three types of books: historical, poetical, and prophetical. Knowing which type of book you are reading is critical to understanding what it says.

In addition to the structure of the Bible, it is important to know the broad strokes of biblical geography. The story told in God's Word is a true story involving real people and real places. Therefore, the better you grasp the locations and relationships between those places, the better you will understand the interactions between peoples and nations. In this session, we will continue to explore the different eras of history in the Old Testament. Are you ready?

SHARE

If you or any of your group members are meeting for the first time, take a few minutes to introduce yourselves. Then jump into the theme of this session by discussing the following:

- What is your favorite section or era of American history? Why?

- Looking back at your notes, what stood out to you in your between-sessions studies that you would like to share with the group?

WATCH

Play the video segment for session two. As you watch, follow along with the main points listed in the outline below and record any key thoughts or concepts that stand out to you.

I. **Review:** There are nine eras in the historical story of the Old Testament: Creation, Patriarch, Exodus, Conquest, Judges, Kingdom, Exile, Return, and Silence.

II. **Geography:** It is important to remember where each story takes place.

    A. The Creation Era is centered in the Garden of Eden.

    B. The Patriarch Era begins in the land of Canaan, which is modern-day Israel.

    C. The Exodus Era largely takes place in Egypt.

    D. The Conquest Era and Judges Era shifts back to Canaan, the promised land for God's people.

    E. The Kingdom Era continues the story of the promised land as a divided nation (North and South).

III. **The Patriarch Era:** God's plan to redeem the world from the consequences of sin began with calling out a people to represent Him on the earth.

A. God called Abraham out of Ur and promised him a land (Canaan), a nation (Israel), and a blessing.

B. Abraham's promises passed to his second son, Isaac.

C. Those promises made to Abraham passed to Isaac's second son, Jacob, whose twelve sons became the leaders of the twelve tribes of Israel.

D. The final patriarch was Joseph, a model of righteousness, who brought his extended family to Egypt.

IV. **The Exodus Era:** There are four parts to the Exodus Era.

A. **Deliverance:** Working through Moses, God miraculously saved His people from slavery in Egypt.

B. **The Law:** God gave Moses the Ten Commandments at Mount Sinai.

C. **Kadesh-Barnea:** Because of their fear, the Israelites refused to follow Moses into the Promised Land, rejecting God's plan.

D. **Wilderness Wandering**: The Israelites wandered in the desert for forty years until the generation that had rejected God died away.

V. **The Conquest Era:** There are also four parts to the Conquest Era.

A. **Jordan:** God led the Israelites back into the promised land by miraculously parting the Jordan River.

B. **Jericho:** Under the command of Joshua, the Israelite army defeated the fortified city of Jericho in Canaan through an unlikely miracle.

C. **Conquest:** Over the course of seven years, the Israelites conquered the people in the land of Canaan and took possession of the promised land.

D. **Dominion:** Each of Israel's twelve tribes was assigned a portion of the promised land to live in and govern.

VI. **The Judges Era:** Recorded in the book of Judges, there are four parts to this era.

A. **Judges:** After Moses and Joshua, the nation of Israel followed political and military leaders called judges.
B. **Rebellion:** Left to their own, the Israelites were spiritually weak and continually chose to rebel against God by worshiping idols.
C. **Cycles:** The Israelites followed a process of sin, discipline, repentance, salvation through a judge, and peace. There are seven of these in the book of Judges.
D. **Ruth:** This short book is set during the Judges Era and tells the story of one of Jesus' ancestors.

VII. **The Kingdom Era:** After the cycle of judges, the Israelites again rebelled against God and demanded a king to lead them. There are four parts to the Kingdom Era.

A. **United Kingdom:** God established a monarchy in Israel through Saul, David, and Solomon.
B. **Divided Kingdom:** A civil war erupted in Israel after Solomon's death, with the nation being split into ten tribes in the north and two in the south.
C. **Northern Kingdom:** Made up of ten tribes, this kingdom rebelled against God for centuries under the rule of many wicked kings.
D. **Southern Kingdom:** Made up of two tribes (Judah and Benjamin), this kingdom bounced between rebellion and righteousness for hundreds of years.

VIII. **Conclusion:** The story of the Israelites reminds us that miracles are not a necessary element for building faith.

    A. The people of Moses' generation saw more miracles than anyone, yet they still rebelled against God.

    B. Because Jesus is the Word of God, we can grow closer to God by faithfully studying and understanding the Bible.

DISCUSS

After watching the video, use the following questions to unpack what you learned as a group.

1. Which of the historical events or eras did you find most the interesting? Why?

_____

_____

_____

_____

_____

2. What questions would you like to have answered after watching the teaching?

_____

_____

_____

_____

_____

_____

3. How can Christians benefit from understanding the history of
    the Jewish people?

    _____

    _____

    _____

    _____

    _____

    _____

    _____

4. How would you describe the Israelites' geographical journey
    from Canaan to Egypt to the wilderness and then back to the
    Promised Land?

    _____

    _____

    _____

    _____

    _____

    _____

    _____

5. The people of the Judges Era lived a continuing cycle of reject-
    ing God, receiving discipline, repenting, and finding peace. How
    can we avoid that cycle as we follow God?

    _____

    _____

    _____

    _____

    _____

    _____

    _____

6. Throughout Israel's history, God's people were heavily influenced by both righteous and wicked kings. How do you see Christians being influenced by the culture today?

_____

_____

_____

_____

_____

_____

APPLY

As we saw in this week's teaching, the fact the Israelites witnessed many miracles did not always increase their faith in God. In fact, the same generation that experienced God's power during the Exodus later chose to reject God's plan at Kadesh-Barnea out of fear. What this means for us is that we don't need to see miracles in order to build a strong faith in God.

Yet it is also true that Christians today witness more miracles than they realize—what we might refer to as "everyday miracles." For example, how often has God answered your prayer in a specific way? How often has God provided exactly what you needed when you needed it? And how much have you changed and grown since your first connection with Christ? These are miracles . . . and they are worth recognizing.

As you close this session, gather with your partner to discuss some of the "everyday miracles" you have experienced in your life. Share about the ways God has provided for you and helped you grow. Once again, commit to keeping track of God's faithfulness in your life and your journey in this study by meeting at least once this week.

BETWEEN-SESSIONS STUDY

Before you begin this personal study, make sure that you have reviewed chapters 5-9 in *30 Days to Understanding the Bible*. Be sure to also read the reflection questions after each activity and make a few notes in your guide about the experience. Once again, there will be a few minutes for you to share any insights you learned at the start of the next session.

DAY 6: THE PATRIARCH ERA

Anyone who has been involved with a family knows they can be filled with both blessings and trials. That was certainly true of the family established during the Patriarch Era of biblical history—a family that eventually grew into the nation of Israel and ultimately produced Jesus Christ, the Savior of the world. We can learn about that family by reading Genesis 12–52. I refer to these chapters as the Patriarch Era because they focus on four key "founding fathers" of the Jewish people: Abraham, Isaac, Jacob, and Joseph.

LAND, PEOPLE, AND BLESSING

After the Fall and the entrance of sin into the world, God enacted a plan for the redemption of humankind. To start that plan, God desired to set apart a people through whom He could work to produce a reflection of Himself—and through whom He could spread the message of redemption to the world. God chose Abraham to be the father of that people. Abraham was living in the land of Ur at the time, which was near the convergence of the Tigris and Euphrates Rivers. But God called Abraham to leave what was familiar and travel to the land of Canaan, which eventually became the promised land for God's chosen people. As we read, God's call to Abraham included not only the promise of land but also of a nation and a worldwide blessing:

> The LORD had said to [Abraham], "Go from your country, your people and your father's household to the land I will show you.
>
> "I will make you into a great nation,
>   and I will bless you;
> I will make your name great,
>   and you will be a blessing.
> I will bless those who bless you,
>   and whoever curses you I will curse;
> and all peoples on earth
>   will be blessed through you" (Genesis 12:1–3).

What sacrifices did Abraham make in order to obey God?

_____

_____

_____

_____

_____

_____

_____

Why were God's promises to Abraham (for land, nation, and blessing) important in the larger story of the Bible?

_____

_____

_____

_____

_____

REVIEW

Write the correct number in the blank from the options on the right. (Refer to the notes you took in the "Watch" portion of this week's group study section if you need additional help.)

NAME		DESCRIPTION
Abraham:		1. Father of the nation of Israel (Genesis 27–35)
Isaac:		2. Leader in Egypt (Genesis 37–50)
Jacob:		3. Father of the Hebrew people (Genesis 12–23)
Joseph:		4. Second father of promise (Genesis 24–26)

DAY 7: THE EXODUS ERA

Think back to the last time you took a trip as part of a family. Can you remember all the packing? All the loading and unloading? Can you recall the different moments of stress, frustration, and delay? If so, then try to imagine what it was like to move an entire *nation* of people several hundred miles in the ancient world.

DELIVERANCE

There were 400 years between Joseph's rule in Egypt and the rise of Moses as a leader. During that time, the Israelites grew from a large family to a large nation with several million members. But also during that time, the Israelites became enslaved to the Egyptians and cried out to God for help. The Lord responded by sending a series of ten plagues to compel the Egyptian pharaoh to let them leave. God then led His people on an incredible journey that lasted more than forty years and encompasses a major portion of the Bible in the books of Exodus—Deuteronomy.

When is a time in your life that you cried out for deliverance? What happened?

_____

_____

_____

_____

When is a time that you have seen God move on your behalf to bring you freedom?

_____

_____

_____

_____

THE LAW

The Exodus Era describes a tremendous journey with both a beginning and an end. The Israelites traveled from Egypt to Canaan, a promised land "flowing with milk and honey." But that journey also included an important stop in the middle. After passing through the Red Sea and witnessing the destruction of Pharaoh's armies, Moses led the Israelites to Mount Sinai. There, the people spent several days camped around the base of the mountain while Moses spoke with God. When Moses returned, he brought what we know as the Ten Commandments, which served as the foundation for Israel's obedience to God throughout the Old Testament.

And God spoke all these words:

"I am the LORD your God, who brought you out of Egypt, out of the land of slavery.

"You shall have no other gods before me.

"You shall not make for yourself an image in the form of anything in heaven above or on the earth beneath or in the waters below. You shall not bow down to them or worship them; for I, the LORD your God, am a jealous God, punishing the children for the sin of the parents to the third and fourth generation of those who hate me, but showing love to a thousand generations of those who love me and keep my commandments.

"You shall not misuse the name of the LORD your God, for the LORD will not hold anyone guiltless who misuses his name.

"Remember the Sabbath day by keeping it holy. Six days you shall labor and do all your work, but the seventh day is a sabbath to the LORD your God. On it you shall not do any work, neither you, nor your son or daughter, nor your male or female servant, nor your animals, nor any foreigner residing in your towns. For in six days the LORD made the heavens and the earth, the sea, and all that is in them, but he rested on the seventh day. Therefore the LORD blessed the Sabbath day and made it holy.

"Honor your father and your mother, so that you may live long in the land the LORD your God is giving you.

"You shall not murder.

"You shall not commit adultery.

"You shall not steal.

"You shall not give false testimony against your neighbor.

"You shall not covet your neighbor's house. You shall not covet your neighbor's wife, or his male or female servant, his ox or donkey, or anything that belongs to your neighbor" (Exodus 20:1–17).

What can we learn about God from these Ten Commandments? How have these commandments influenced your life?

_____

_____

_____

_____

_____

Why is there value in understanding the Israelites' failures during the Exodus Era, including their failure to follow these commandments?

_____

_____

_____

_____

_____

_____

KADESH-BARNEA AND THE WILDERNESS

The Israelites left Mount Sinai and migrated north to Kadesh-Barnea, the southern gateway into the Promised Land. Once there, Moses sent twelve spies to investigate the land. Ten of the spies reported there were hostile enemies that were too great for the Israelites to overcome. Two of the spies, Joshua and Caleb, urged the people to believe in God for the victory. But the Israelites believed the majority report, and as a consequence they were forced to wander in the wilderness for forty years, until the rebellious generation had died out.

What do these events tell us about taking God at His word?

_____

_____

_____

_____

_____

When are some times that God has called you to step out in faith? What happened as a result?

_____

_____

_____

_____

_____

REVIEW

Write the correct number in the blank from the options on the right. (Refer to the notes you took in the "Watch" portion of this week's group study section if you need additional help.)

SUBJECT	DESCRIPTION
Deliverance:	1. God's commandments at Mount Sinai (Exodus 19–40)
The Law:	2. Place of rebellion against God (Numbers 10–14)
Kadesh-Barnea:	3. Consequences of rebellion (Numbers 20–36)
Wandering:	4. Freedom from slavery in Egypt (Numbers 20–36)

DAY 8: THE CONQUEST ERA

As we have seen, not everyone among the Israelites cowered in fear when faced with the military strength of the people in the Promised Land. Joshua, one of the twelve spies sent to observe the land, was firm in his belief that the Israelites would be victorious. "Do not rebel against the LORD," he said. "And do not be afraid of the people of the land, because we will devour them" (Numbers 14:9). Joshua was ultimately chosen to lead God's people after the forty years of wandering had ended. He was the leader who finally led the Israelites into the Promised Land during the Conquest Era of biblical history.

THE CONQUEST

It's hard to overstate the difficulty of Joshua's position. For one thing, he was following in the footsteps of Moses—one of the greatest leaders in history. For another, he was about to engage a military conflict against several groups who lived in fortified cities and commanded terrifying armies. Yet Joshua was not alone. God Himself spoke to him and offered a series of commands and promises that inspired not only him but also the entire nation.

After the death of Moses the servant of the LORD, the LORD said to Joshua son of Nun, Moses' aide: "Moses my servant is dead. Now then, you and all these people, get ready to cross the Jordan River into the land I am about to give to them—to the Israelites. I will give you every place where you set your foot, as I promised Moses. Your territory will extend from the desert to Lebanon, and from the great river, the Euphrates—all the Hittite country—to the Mediterranean Sea in the west. No one will be able to stand against you all the days of your life. As I was with Moses, so I will be with you; I will never leave you nor forsake you. Be strong and courageous, because you will lead these people to inherit the land I swore to their ancestors to give them.

"Be strong and very courageous. Be careful to obey all the law my servant Moses gave you; do not turn from it to the right or to the left, that you may be successful wherever you go. Keep this Book of the Law always on your lips; meditate on it day and night, so that you may be careful to do everything written in it. Then you will be prosperous and successful. Have I not commanded you? Be strong and courageous. Do not be afraid; do not be discouraged, for the LORD your God will be with you wherever you go" (Joshua 1:1–9).

How should we understand God's command for violent conquest both in these verses and throughout the Old Testament?

_____

_____

_____

_____

What are some ways the Israelites' dominion of the Promised Land set the stage for other major events in the Bible?

_____

_____

_____

_____

_____

_____

_____

_____

REVIEW

Write the correct number in the blank from the options on the right. (Refer to the notes you took in the "Watch" portion of this week's group study section if you need additional help.)

SUBJECT		DESCRIPTION
Jordan:		1. The defeat of Canaan (Joshua 7–12)
Jericho:		2. A miraculous parting of water (Joshua 1–5)
Conquest:		3. Finalizing the taking of Canaan (Joshua 13–20)
Dominion:		4. Miraculous conquest of a city (Joshua 6)

DAY 9: THE JUDGES ERA

When we hear the word *judge* today, we think of a legal judge in a long, black robe presiding over a courtroom. In the ancient world, however, the concept of a judge was more synonymous with that of a leader outside of a monarchy. This was the case with the leaders highlighted in the Judges Era of biblical history. The most famous of Israel's judges would have to be Samson, the strong man with long hair and little self-control. Other major judges from this era include Gideon, who defeated an army of thousands with only 300 men, and Samuel, a transitional figure who was both the last judge and the first prophet.

A STANDOUT FROM THE REST

Another major judge of the time, who stood out from the others, was a woman named Deborah. It has often been said within the church that women were treated as second-class citizens in the ancient world. While this is true in many ways, it is also true that the Bible is filled with women who were valued and respected leaders within their communities. For instance, the book of Ruth is contained within the Judges Era, and Ruth herself is a shining example of righteousness—so much so that she is an ancestor of Jesus Christ. Deborah was another valued and respected woman of the era, and she was a powerhouse in many ways.

> Again the Israelites did evil in the eyes of the LORD. . . . So the LORD sold them into the hands of Jabin king of Canaan, who reigned in Hazor. Sisera, the commander of his army, was based in Harosheth Haggoyim. Because he had nine hundred chariots fitted with iron and had cruelly oppressed the Israelites for twenty years, they cried to the Lord for help.
>
> Now Deborah, a prophet, the wife of Lappidoth, was leading Israel at that time. She held court under the Palm of Deborah between Ramah and Bethel in the hill country of Ephraim, and the Israelites went up to her

to have their disputes decided. She sent for Barak son of Abinoam from Kedesh in Naphtali and said to him, "The Lord, the God of Israel, commands you: 'Go, take with you ten thousand men of Naphtali and Zebulun and lead them up to Mount Tabor. I will lead Sisera, the commander of Jabin's army, with his chariots and his troops to the Kishon River and give him into your hands'" (Judges 4:1-7).

How do you see the cycle in Judges of sin, discipline, repentance, and peace in this passage?

_____

_____

_____

_____

_____

Where do you see the value of leadership highlighted in the Bible? In your own life?

_____

_____

_____

_____

REVIEW

Write the correct number in the blank from the options on the right. (Refer to the notes you took in the "Watch" portion of this week's group study section if you need additional help.)

SUBJECT	DESCRIPTION
Judges:	1. A model woman
Rebellion:	2. The leaders of Israel
Cycles:	3. The breaking of God's law
Ruth:	4. Repetition of Israel's misfortunes

DAY 10: THE KINGDOM ERA

Freedom always comes with a price. The kings of Israel wanted complete freedom. They wanted the freedom to ignore the directives God had given them on how to rule and wage war. At the same time, they wanted the freedom to have economic and military prosperity. As a result, the Kingdom Era was a turbulent time for God's people. When a righteous king ruled, the nation prospered. When an unrighteous king gained the throne, the nation faltered.

UNITED KINGDOM

God allowed Samuel, the last judge, to anoint a man named Saul to be the first king of a united Israel. Saul did not prove to be a righteous king, so God soon removed him and called another man to serve as the leader of His people. The prophet Samuel anointed a shepherd named David to take his place, rather than Saul's son Jonathan. David was not a perfect man, yet God Himself described him as "a man after my own heart" (Acts 13:22). Because of David's humility and integrity, God made him an incredible promise that is still in effect today:

> This is what the LORD Almighty says: I took you from
> the pasture, from tending the flock, and appointed you

ruler over my people Israel. I have been with you wherever you have gone, and I have cut off all your enemies from before you. Now I will make your name great, like the names of the greatest men on earth. And I will provide a place for my people Israel and will plant them so that they can have a home of their own and no longer be disturbed. Wicked people will not oppress them anymore, as they did at the beginning and have done ever since the time I appointed leaders over my people Israel. I will also give you rest from all your enemies.

The LORD declares to you that the LORD himself will establish a house for you: When your days are over and you rest with your ancestors, I will raise up your offspring to succeed you, your own flesh and blood, and I will establish his kingdom. He is the one who will build a house for my Name, and I will establish the throne of his kingdom forever. I will be his father, and he will be my son. When he does wrong, I will punish him with a rod wielded by men, with floggings inflicted by human hands. But my love will never be taken away from him, as I took it away from Saul, whom I removed from before you. Your house and your kingdom will endure forever before me; your throne will be established forever (2 Samuel 7:8–16).

What can we learn from these verses about how kings were supposed to lead and what God intended Israel's kings to accomplish?

_____

_____

_____

_____

God promised that David's house and kingdom would "endure for-ever." Why is that a critical promise within the pages of Scripture?

_____

_____

_____

_____

_____

_____

DIVIDED KINGDOM

When David died, the throne of Israel passed to his son Solo-mon. However, as a result of his spiritual drifting, a civil war erupted after his death. Jeroboam rose up and led ten of the tribes to break off and form the northern kingdom of Israel. He was an unrighteous man, as were the nineteen kings that fol-lowed him, and ultimately God delivered them into the hands of the Assyrians, where they were assimilated into the culture. The two tribes that remained under Rehoboam, the son of Solomon, formed the southern kingdom of Judah. This kingdom lasted for 400 years, due to the rule of eight righteous kings (out of twenty), but ultimately God had to bring judgment on it as well. Judah was captured by the Babylonians and taken into exile.

What were the consequences of Solomon not following the Lord?

_____

_____

_____

_____

_____

_____

Why do you think God allowed Judah to last for so much longer than Israel?

_____

_____

_____

_____

_____

REVIEW

Write the correct number in the blank from the options on the right. (Refer to the notes you took in the "Watch" portion of this week's group study section if you need additional help.)

EVENT		DESCRIPTION
United Kingdom:		1. Completely unrighteous kingdom (2 Kings)
Divided Kingdom:		2. A new monarchy (1 & 2 Samuel)
Northern Kingdom:		3. Inconsistent kingdom (2 Kings)
Southern Kingdom:		4. A civil war (1 Kings)

Fill in the blanks from memory:

ERA	SUMMARY
Creation:	Adam is created by God, but he _____ This is known as "the _____." This destroys God's original _____ for humans.
Patriarch:	Abraham is _____ by God to leave his own country and "father" a new _____.
Exodus:	Through Moses, the Hebrew people are _____ from slavery in the land of _____.

Conquest:	Joshua leads the _____ of the _____ _____.
Judges:	A group of leaders known as the _____ were chosen to _____ the Israelites for 400 rebellious years.
Kingdom:	David is the greatest king in the _____ Kingdom, but after his death there is a split between the Kingdom of _____ in the north and the Kingdom of _____ in the south.

APPLY

Check in with your partner at least once this week to review what you studied. Use the following questions to help cement the main concepts in your minds.

- **Patriarch Era:** Abraham's obedience resulted in the entire world being blessed. What is something God has recently commanded you to do? What is required of you to obey His call?

- **Exodus Era:** Talk through the Ten Commandments. Share any ways that you have struggled with any of these commands. Pray for one another as you continue this journey of understanding the Bible.

- **Conquest Era:** Take a moment to discuss a few people who need your encouragement today. Commit to sending them a quick note—text, email, or letter—to let them know you are in their corner.

- **Judges Era:** Talk about some leaders who have been significant in your life. Who do you currently turn to for guidance and advice? Where do you currently have opportunities to serve as a leader for others?

- **Kingdom Era:** One of the reasons David was considered a man after God's own heart is that he understood the value of worship. With this in mind, share a psalm, prayer, or passage that has been especially meaningful to you in your worship to God.

FOR NEXT WEEK

Use the space below to write any insights or questions from your personal study that you want to discuss at the next group meeting. In preparation for next week, review chapters 10–14 in *30 Days to Understanding the Bible*.

THE LATER HISTORY OF ISRAEL

EXILE — SILENCE ERAS

God will forgive whoever comes to Him for repentance.
But as the later history of Israel reveals, this doesn't change
the fact that sin has consequences. God forgives the man for
jumping off the building, but God's laws of gravity dictates that
the man will still fall to the ground.

MAX ANDERS

WELCOME

Welcome to the third group session for *30 Days to Understanding the Bible*. Up to this point, we have focused primarily on the historical books of the Old Testament. We examined how God demonstrated His power in the Creation Era. We saw how He called out a special people for His purposes in the Patriarch Era. We witnessed Him rescuing those people from slavery in the Exodus Era and leading them into the Promised Land in the Conquest Era. We then saw how those people often failed to live in obedience to Him in the Judges Era and Kingdom Era.

This week, we will conclude our overview of biblical history in the Old Testament by examining the consequences of that disobedience in the Exile Era. But we will also see God's mercy at work in the Return Era and the Silence Era. We will also explore the broad strokes of the poetical books and prophetical books of the Old Testament—two types of biblical literature that contain many applications for believers in Christ today.

This means by the end of this week, we will be halfway through our journey toward biblical understanding and ready to move on to the New Testament. Let's get started!

SHARE

Jump into the theme of this session by discussing the following questions:

- The Bible contains not only many stories but also many different kinds of literature. What types of literature do you like best? Why?

- Looking back at your notes, what stood out to you in your between-sessions studies that you would like to share with the group?

WATCH

Play the video segment for session three. As you watch, follow along with the main points listed in the outline below and record any key thoughts or concepts that stand out to you.

I. **Review:** Geography is a critical part of understanding biblical history.

    A. The Creation Era covers the beginning of all things, including our world.

    B. The Patriarch Era begins in Canaan—the "promised land" for the Israelites, which is also present-day Israel.

    C. The Exodus Era starts with God's people struggling as slaves in Egypt and then moves out into the wilderness of the Middle East.

    D. The Conquest Era, Judges Era, and Kingdom Era are all centered once again in Canaan, the Promised Land.

    E. The geography of the Exile Era will take place mainly in Babylon, which is later conquered by Persia.

    F. The Return Era and the Silence Era will again focus on the land of Canaan.

II. **The Exile Era:** The guiding principle of the historical books is that God promised to bless His people if they obeyed Him but said that He would discipline if they rejected Him. The Israelites' failure led to their exile, of which there were four subdivisions.

    A. **Prophecy:** God sent prophets to warn both the Northern and Southern Kingdoms about their upcoming destruction. These men of God prophesied that the exile would last for seventy years.

B. **Prophets:** Prophets such as Daniel and Ezekiel were key leaders among God's people during the time of the exile.

C. **Exiles:** The exiles from the Southern Kingdom (Judah) were assimilated into Babylon's culture, yet they retained their Jewish identity.

D. **Power Change:** The nation of Babylon was conquered by Persia, which set the stage for the Israelite people to return to their homeland.

III. **The Return Era:** After seventy years, God's people were allowed to return to the Promised Land. This era has four parts.

A. **Disrepair:** The city of Jerusalem was destroyed during Babylon's final attack. The city fell into disrepair during the seventy years of exile.

B. **Temple:** Through King Cyrus of Persia, God commanded that the temple in Jerusalem be rebuilt. Zerubbabel was the leader of this effort in Jerusalem.

C. **People:** While Zerubbabel rebuilt the temple in Jerusalem, a scribe named Ezra rebuilt God's people by reteaching them God's laws.

D. **Walls** Jerusalem would never be safe from enemies while its walls were broken, so God called Nehemiah to lead their reconstruction.

IV. **The Silence Era:** With no written revelation from God for more than 400 years, the Silence Era has four parts.

A. **The Changing of the Guard:** Just as the empire of Babylon was defeated by Persia, the Persian Empire was overthrown by the Greeks under Alexander the Great, and the Greeks were defeated by Rome.

B. **Political Sects:** During the silent years, many Jews organized into different political and military groups, including the Zealots and the Maccabaeans.

C. **Religious Sects:** The Jews also divided into religious groups, including the Pharisees and Sadducees.

D. **Messianic Hope:** The Messiah had been prophesied throughout the Old Testament as a Savior, which is what the Jews needed during the Silence Era.

V. **Poetical Books:** There are five books in the Old Testament that were written as wisdom literature (poems and songs).

A. **Job:** A story of spiritual warfare, Job was a righteous man who lost everything. His story helps explore the reality of suffering.

B. **Psalms:** A collection of songs that served as a hymnal and book of prayer for the Israelites.

C. **Proverbs:** A collection of short, pity maxims intended to help the reader find wisdom for everyday life.

D. **Ecclesiastes:** Written primarily by King Solomon, the book explores questions surrounding the meaning of life.

E. **Song of Solomon:** Also written by Solomon, this book serves as God's marriage manual.

VI. **Prophetical Books:** These books, written after the kingdom of Israel was divided, span a timeline of several hundred years. They include four primary themes.

A. **Major and Minor Prophets:** The longer prophetical books are called "major," while the shorter are "minor."

B. **Time Periods of the Prophets:** Most of the prophetical books were written before the exile as a warning to God's people. Others were written during and after the exile.

C. **Foretelling:** The prophetical books are famous for including prophecies about the future, which were given to the prophets by God.

D. **Forthtelling:** The majority of the content in the prophetical books was proclaiming God's Word and will to people in their current day.

VII. **Conclusion:** The content of the Old Testament points forward to Jesus as the Messiah and Savior of the world.

A. A key lesson from the Old Testament is that we should obey God in all things.

B. Another key lesson is that disobedience and sin always produce consequences.

DISCUSS

After watching the video, use the following questions to unpack what you learned as a group.

1. What questions would you like to have answered after watching the teaching?

2. One of the guiding principles of the historical books is that *if Israel had trusted God and obeyed Him, God would have richly blessed them—but since they rejected Him, the Lord responded with discipline.* How does this principle still apply today?

3. What are some key lessons from the history of the Israelites that we should learn and follow as Christians today?

4. How have you been impacted by the psalms, proverbs, and other wisdom literature of the Old Testament?

5. The prophets revealed God's word and will to the people of Israel. What are the ways that God guides and instructs us today?

    _____

    _____

    _____

    _____

    _____

6. What has surprised you most during this journey through the "fourteeners" of the Old Testament? Why?

    _____

    _____

    _____

    _____

    _____

APPLY

Trust is a concept that can be difficult to quantify. It is easy to *say* that we trust another person, but how do we actually *measure* that trust? In the same way, it is easy for us as Christians to declare that we trust in God—but how can we determine whether that trust is real?

An answer can be found by connecting our *trust* in God to *obedience*. The more we trust in God's power and God's plan, the more we will obey what God asks us to do. The less we trust God, the more we will try to retain control over our own lives.

As you close this session, gather with your partner to talk about obedience. Discuss where you might have opportunities to obey God this week, what obstacles could hinder or prevent you from obeying Him, and what you will do to overcome those obstacles and express your trust in God through your actions.

BETWEEN-SESSIONS STUDY

Before you begin this personal study, make sure that you have reviewed chapters 10–14 in *30 Days to Understanding the Bible*. Be sure to also read the reflection questions after each activity and make a few notes in your guide about the experience. Once again, there will be a few minutes for you to share any insights you learned at the start of the next session.

DAY 11: THE EXILE ERA

Forgiveness is one of the greatest gifts that we can receive. When we sin, we are rebelling against God—just as Adam and Eve did in the Garden of Eden. However, because God loves us, He has made a way for our sins to be forgiven through the death and resurrection of Christ. What an incredible blessing! We are not defined by our mistakes and failures. We can turn back to God, who has promised forgiveness to all who repent. Forgiveness is at the core of our relationship with God. Even so, it is important for us to remember that sin has consequences.

UNHEEDED WARNINGS

The Israelites tasted this bitter reality. Their relationship with God deteriorated after the reigns of David and Solomon. The people lived in roller-coaster rebellion for 400 years, during which time God sent numerous prophets to warn them—warnings that were generally unheeded. Eventually, the northern kingdom fell to the Assyrians in 722 BC, and its people were carried away into captivity and assimilated. The prophet Jeremiah warned the same would happen to the southern kingdom of Judah if they did not change their ways, but they also failed to listen. As a consequence, they were carried into captivity by the Babylonians in 586 BC. However, this time God decreed they would be preserved as a race and return to their homeland.

> This is what the LORD says: "When seventy years are completed for Babylon, I will come to you and fulfill my good promise to bring you back to this place. For I know the plans I have for you," declares the LORD, "plans to prosper you and not to harm you, plans to give you hope and a future. Then you will call on me and come and pray to me, and I will listen to you. You will seek me and find me when you seek me with all your heart. I will be found by you," declares the LORD, "and will bring you back from captivity. I will gather you from all the nations and places where I have banished you," declares the LORD, "and will bring you back to the place from which I carried you into exile" (Jeremiah 29:10–14).

Why do you think the Israelites failed to heed God's warnings through the prophets?

_____

_____

_____

_____

_____

_____

What promise did God make to His people regarding their captivity?

_____

_____

_____

_____

_____

_____

_____

_____

_____

_____

_____

_____

LIVING IN EXILE

As we have just seen, the Lord still had plans to preserve His people as a race, even though they had now been carried into exile in Babylon. During the seventy years of captivity, He sent other prophets, such as Daniel and Ezekiel, to encourage them to remain faithful to Him. Ezekiel foretold of a national restoration, while Daniel demonstrated what it meant to stay true to God while living in a foreign land and experiencing persecution. Daniel also witnessed the conquest of Babylonia by the Persians, who would ultimately allow the exiles to return to their homeland.

[Daniel said,] "Your Majesty, the Most High God gave your father Nebuchadnezzar sovereignty and greatness and glory and splendor. Because of the high position he gave him, all the nations and peoples of every language dreaded and feared him. . . . But when his heart became arrogant and hardened with pride, he was deposed from his royal throne and stripped of his glory.

He was driven away from people and given the mind of an animal; he lived with the wild donkeys and ate grass like the ox; and his body was drenched with the dew of heaven, until he acknowledged that the Most High God is sovereign over all kingdoms on earth and sets over them anyone he wishes.

"But you, Belshazzar, his son, have not humbled yourself, though you knew all this. Instead, you have set yourself up against the Lord of heaven. You had the goblets from his temple brought to you, and you and your nobles, your wives and your concubines drank wine from them. You praised the gods of silver and gold, of bronze, iron, wood and stone, which cannot see or hear or understand. But you did not honor the God who holds in his hand your life and all your ways. Therefore he sent the hand that wrote the inscription.

"This is the inscription that was written: MENE, MENE, TEKEL, PARSIN.

"Here is what these words mean:

MENE: God has numbered the days of your reign and brought it to an end.

TEKEL: You have been weighed on the scales and found wanting.

PERES: Your kingdom is divided and given to the Medes and Persians."

Then at Belshazzar's command, Daniel was clothed in purple, a gold chain was placed around his neck, and he was proclaimed the third highest ruler in the kingdom.

That very night Belshazzar, king of the Babylonians, was slain, and Darius the Mede took over the kingdom, at the age of sixty-two (Daniel 5:18–31).

Why is Israel's rebellion against God such an important theme throughout the Old Testament?

_____

_____

_____

_____

_____

Where do you see the connection between sin and consequences in the world today?

_____

_____

_____

_____

_____

REVIEW

Write the correct number in the blank from the options on the right. (Refer to the notes you took in the "Watch" portion of this week's group study section if you need additional help.)

SUBJECT		DESCRIPTION
Prophecy:		1. The Persian Empire conquers Babylon (Daniel 4)
Prophets:		2. Assimilated into the culture (Daniel 1)
Exiles:		3. Warning of impending captivity (Jeremiah 34:1–3)
Power Change:		4. Encouraging faithfulness among the exiles (Ezekiel 40–48)

DAY 12: THE RETURN ERA

You have likely heard the saying, "you can never go home again," but that wasn't true for the Israelites. After seventy years of exile, as God promised, the captives from Judah were allowed to return to their native home—specifically the city of Jerusalem. This was the good news. The bad news was that Jerusalem had been devasted during the conquest and by decades of neglect. The temple had been destroyed, the city walls were broken down, and the infrastructure needed for maintaining a functional government had been lost.

REBUILDING THE TEMPLE AND THE PEOPLE

God prompted Cyrus, the king of Persia, to initiate the financing for the rebuilding of the temple in Jerusalem. The rebuilding had begun under Zerubbabel, but stalled under opposition from the people who had settled in and around Jerusalem. At the urging of the prophets Haggai and Zechariah, the restoration was completed. A priest named Ezra then led the spiritual rebuilding of the people, instituting a national re-education program to instruct them in God's laws.

> In the first year of Cyrus king of Persia, in order to fulfill the word of the Lord spoken by Jeremiah, the Lord moved the heart of Cyrus king of Persia to make a proclamation throughout his realm and also to put it in writing:
> "This is what Cyrus king of Persia says:
> "'The LORD, the God of heaven, has given me all the kingdoms of the earth and he has appointed me to build a temple for him at Jerusalem in Judah. Any of his people among you may go up to Jerusalem in Judah and build the temple of the LORD, the God of Israel, the God who is in Jerusalem, and may their God be with them. And in

any locality where survivors may now be living, the people are to provide them with silver and gold, with goods and livestock, and with freewill offerings for the temple of God in Jerusalem'" (Ezra 1:1–4).

What are some ways that the events of the Return Era displayed God's power?

_____

_____

_____

_____

_____

When has God blessed you with the opportunity for a second chance?

_____

_____

_____

_____

HOPE IS RESTORED

Many of the captives had now returned to their homeland and had rebuilt the temple. However, the walls of the city of Jerusalem were still in ruin—which posed not only a security threat but was also a source of national humiliation. In response, a man named Nehemiah compelled another Persian king (named Artaxerxes) to finance the rebuilding effort. A short time later, Nehemiah reports how the walls were rebuilt and the restoration was completed—even in the face of threats and opposition from their enemies.

When word came to Sanballat, Tobiah, Geshem the Arab and the rest of our enemies that I had rebuilt the wall and not a gap was left in it—though up to that time I had not set the doors in the gates—Sanballat and Geshem sent me this message: "Come, let us meet together in one of the villages on the plain of Ono."

But they were scheming to harm me; so I sent messengers to them with this reply: "I am carrying on a great project and cannot go down. Why should the work stop while I leave it and go down to you?" Four times they sent me the same message, and each time I gave them the same answer. . . .

They were all trying to frighten us, thinking, "Their hands will get too weak for the work, and it will not be completed."

But I prayed, "Now strengthen my hands." . . .

Remember Tobiah and Sanballat, my God, because of what they have done; remember also the prophet Noadiah and how she and the rest of the prophets have been trying to intimidate me. So the wall was completed on the twenty-fifth of Elul, in fifty-two days (Nehemiah 6:1–4, 9, 14–15).

Why was the Israelites' return to Jerusalem a significant event in light of biblical history?

_____

_____

_____

_____

_____

_____

How has God led you through a time of opposition in your life?

_____

_____

_____

_____

_____

_____

REVIEW

Write the correct number in the blank from the options on the right. (Refer to the notes you took in the "Watch" portion of this week's group study section if you need additional help.)

SUBJECT	DESCRIPTION
Disrepair:	1. Spiritual rebuilding (Ezra 7–10)
Temple:	2. Rebuilding the temple (Ezra 1–6)
People:	3. Destruction from war and neglect (Nehemiah 1:1–3)
Walls:	4. Restoration complete (Nehemiah 2–13)

DAY 13: THE SILENCE ERA

When you think about it, much of history exists as the time between significant events. For example, what we know of as the Cold War is basically the period of time between the end of World War II in 1946 and the collapse of the Soviet Union in

1989. In a similar way, the Silence Era is the period between the reconstruction of Jerusalem and the birth of John the Baptist in the New Testament. There is a long stretch of time between those moments—roughly 400 years. Many things happened during those centuries, and many were important within the story of the Israelites. However, we refer to this period as the Silence Era because it contained no recorded revelation from God. He was silent . . . and His people waited.

MESSIANIC HOPE

For what were God's people waiting? Among other things, they longed for a *Savior*—the one whom God had promised would defeat evil and restore His kingdom on the earth. The Israelites referred to this promised king as the *Messiah*, and the four centuries of the Silence Era were packed with an ever-increasing hope that He would come—and come soon. Malachi is the final book in the Old Testament, and it is packed with promises and prophecies about who the Messiah would be and what He would accomplish on earth.

> "I will send my messenger, who will prepare the way before me. Then suddenly the Lord you are seeking will come to his temple; the messenger of the covenant, whom you desire, will come," says the LORD Almighty.
>
> But who can endure the day of his coming? Who can stand when he appears? For he will be like a refiner's fire or a launderer's soap. He will sit as a refiner and purifier of silver; he will purify the Levites and refine them like gold and silver. Then the LORD will have men who will bring offerings in righteousness, and the offerings of Judah and Jerusalem will be acceptable to the LORD, as in days gone by, as in former years. . . .

"Surely the day is coming; it will burn like a furnace. All the arrogant and every evildoer will be stubble, and the day that is coming will set them on fire," says the LORD Almighty. "Not a root or a branch will be left to them. But for you who revere my name, the sun of righteousness will rise with healing in its rays. And you will go out and frolic like well-fed calves. Then you will trample on the wicked; they will be ashes under the soles of your feet on the day when I act," says the LORD Almighty (Malachi 3:1–4; 4:1–3).

How do these passages' depiction of the Messiah compare and contrast to what you know of Jesus' life and ministry?

_____

_____

_____

_____

_____

When have you gone through a season where it felt as if God was silent in your life?

_____

_____

_____

_____

REVIEW

Write the correct number in the blank from the options on the right. (Refer to the notes you took in the "Watch" portion of this week's group study section if you need additional help.)

SUBJECT	DESCRIPTION
The Changing Guard:	1. Pharisees and Sadducees
Political Sects:	2. The march of nations
Religious Sects:	3. Expectations of a savior
Messianic Hope:	4. Maccabaeans and Zealots

DAY 14: POETICAL BOOKS

Throughout recorded history, wisdom literature has been a core element of human cultures. We express who we are through our stories, our songs, our poems, and our aphorisms. The same was true of the ancient Israelites—the people through whom God chose to reveal Himself to the world. The Poetical Books in the Bible—which include Job, Psalms, Proverbs, Ecclesiastes, and the Song of Solomon—can be located in the timeline constructed by the Historical Books. The book of Job was written during the time of the events of Genesis. The Psalms were recorded during the life of David depicted in 2 Samuel. The books of Proverbs, Ecclesiastes, and Song of Solomon were written during the lifetime of Solomon depicted in 1 Kings.

SONGS OF SUFFERING AND OF PRAISE

The book of Job depicts the events that took place in a godly man's life when his health, his wealth, and family are suddenly taken from him. The book is structured in a series of debates between Job and his friends as they wrestle with the idea of suffering and God's sovereignty. In the end, Job can only conclude, "I know that you can do all things . . . I spoke of things I did not understand, things too wonderful for me to know" (Job 42:2–3).

The book of Psalms is a collection of 150 "songs" that are divided into five smaller books. The word *psalm* originally meant "to strike the strings of an instrument," and this term became synonymous with praise. The Psalms were used as a book of prayer and praise in public worship in the tabernacle, temple, and synagogues. There are three primary types of psalms: praise, thanksgiving, and lament. King David, who wrote almost half of the psalms that in the Bible, was a master of both literary technique and emotional expression, as the following passage relates.

> The law of the LORD is perfect,
>> refreshing the soul.
> The statutes of the LORD are trustworthy,
>> making wise the simple.
> The precepts of the LORD are right,
>> giving joy to the heart.
> The commands of the LORD are radiant,
>> giving light to the eyes.
> The fear of the LORD is pure,
>> enduring forever.
> The decrees of the LORD are firm,
>> and all of them are righteous.
>
> They are more precious than gold,
>> than much pure gold;
> they are sweeter than honey,
>> than honey from the honeycomb.
> By them your servant is warned;
>> in keeping them there is great reward.
> But who can discern their own errors?
>> Forgive my hidden faults.

Keep your servant also from willful sins;
    may they not rule over me.
Then I will be blameless,
    innocent of great transgression.

May these words of my mouth and this meditation
    of my heart
be pleasing in your sight,
    Lord, my Rock and my Redeemer (Psalm 19:7–14).

What emotions do you experience when you read these verses?

_____

_____

_____

_____

How is this psalm similar to songs and poems that you have encountered in today's culture? How is it different?

_____

_____

_____

_____

THE WISDOM OF SOLOMON

King Solomon is widely regarded as the wisest person in history—and we have access to that wisdom through three books that he wrote in the Bible. While many "wise" people are often vague or flowery in their writings, Solomon's words are both practical and useful. In other words, the writings of Solomon are wisdom applied to daily life.

The book of Proverbs is packed with aphorisms and instructions that cover a wide spectrum of life experiences. The purpose of these proverbs is to impart *wisdom* on the reader or *skill for living*. The book known as Song of Solomon (or Song of Songs) is a manual for godly marriages—quite a practical topic! The book of Ecclesiastes is Solomon's study of human existence and his answer to the question, "What is the meaning of life?" Here is a brief look at this "applied wisdom" of Solomon from this book.

There is a time for everything,

> and a season for every activity under the heavens:
> a time to be born and a time to die,
> a time to plant and a time to uproot,
> a time to kill and a time to heal,
> a time to tear down and a time to build,
> a time to weep and a time to laugh,
> a time to mourn and a time to dance,
> a time to scatter stones and a time to gather them,
> a time to embrace and a time to refrain
>   from embracing,
> a time to search and a time to give up,
> a time to keep and a time to throw away,
> a time to tear and a time to mend,
> a time to be silent and a time to speak,
> a time to love and a time to hate,
> a time for war and a time for peace.

What do workers gain from their toil? I have seen the burden God has laid on the human race. He has made everything beautiful in its time. He has also set eternity in the human heart; yet no one can fathom what God has done from beginning to end. I know that there is nothing better for people than to be happy and to do good while they live. That each of them may eat and drink, and find satisfaction in all their toil—this is the gift of God (Ecclesiastes 3:1–13).

How have you seen Solomon's statement proven true that God "set eternity in the human heart"?

_____

_____

_____

_____

_____

What have you found to be effective when it comes to applying biblical wisdom to your everyday life?

_____

_____

_____

_____

REVIEW

Write the correct number in the blank from the options on the right. (Refer to the notes you took in the "Watch" portion of this week's group study section if you need additional help.)

BOOK		DESCRIPTION
Job:		1. Futility of temporal pursuits
Psalms:		2. Suffering and God's sovereignty
Proverbs:		3. God's marriage manual
Ecclesiastes:		4. Praise in public worship
Song of Solomon:		5. Wisdom / skill for living

DAY 15: PROPHETICAL BOOKS

What comes to mind when you hear the word *prophecy*? Most people think of a person declaring, perhaps in cryptic language, events that will take place years or even centuries later. This kind of prophecy is called "foretelling," and there are certainly many examples in the Old Testament where one of God's prophets accurately predicted future events. However, another more common form of prophecy that we find in the Bible is called "forthtelling," which is the act of declaring God's message to those who will listen. This is primarily what we find in the Old Testament—the prophets proclaiming the Word of God to the people of their day.

MESSIANIC PROPHECY

The Old Testament prophets had no power in and of themselves. Their ability to speak truth—and especially their ability to predict the future—were based in God's power alone. In fact, it was known among the Israelites that if a prophet declared something that was proven untrue, that person was in no way connected to God. Such *false* prophets were to be put to death to keep pure the ranks of God's *true* prophets. To this end, one of the most famous *true* prophecies in the Bible concerns the death of the Messiah as a sacrificial offering for all people. It is found in the book of Isaiah, which was written 700 years before the birth of Jesus.

> He grew up before him like a tender shoot,
>   and like a root out of dry ground.
> He had no beauty or majesty to attract us to him,
>   nothing in his appearance that we should desire him.
> He was despised and rejected by mankind,
>   a man of suffering, and familiar with pain.

Like one from whom people hide their faces
    he was despised, and we held him in low esteem.

Surely he took up our pain
    and bore our suffering,
yet we considered him punished by God,
    stricken by him, and afflicted.
But he was pierced for our transgressions,
    he was crushed for our iniquities;
the punishment that brought us peace was on him,
    and by his wounds we are healed.
We all, like sheep, have gone astray,
    each of us has turned to our own way;
and the Lord has laid on him
    the iniquity of us all (Isaiah 53:2–6).

In what ways did Jesus' death fulfill the prophecies contained in these verses?

_____

_____

_____

_____

What are some possible reasons why God included prophecies about the future within the biblical text? What do those prophecies achieve?

_____

_____

_____

_____

_____

REVIEW

Write the correct number in the blank from the options on the right.

SUBJECT		
Designation:		1. Predicting the future
Time Period:		2. Proclaiming God's teachings
Foretelling:		3. Pre-Exile, Exile, Post-Exile
Forthtelling:		4. Major and Minor Prophets

Fill in the blanks from memory:

ERA	SUMMARY
Creation:	Adam is created by God, but he _____. This is known as "the _____." This destroys God's original _____ for humans.
Patriarch:	Abraham is _____ by God to leave his own country and "father" a new _____.
Exodus:	Through Moses, the Hebrew people are _____ from slavery in the land of _____.
Conquest:	Joshua leads the _____ of the _____ _____.
Judges:	A group of leaders known as the _____ were chosen to _____ the Israelites for 400 rebellious years.
Kingdom:	David is the greatest king in the _____ Kingdom, but after his death there is a split between the Kingdom of _____ in the north and the Kingdom of _____ in the south.
Exile:	The rebellion of Judah and Israel leads to their _____ by outside powers and the _____ of the Jewish people.
Return:	God allows the captives to return to the city of _____, where they rebuild the temple, the city _____ under Nehemiah, and are reinstructed in God's _____ by leaders such as Ezra.
Silence:	During these years, the Jews organize into different political groups, including the _____ and the _____, and different religious groups, including the _____ and the _____.

APPLY

Check in with your partner at least once this week to review what you studied. Use the following questions to help cement the main concepts in your minds.

- **Exile Era:** Jesus said, "Ask the Lord of the harvest . . . to send out workers into his harvest field" (Luke 10:2). Pray for God to raise up women and men like the Old Testament prophets to declare the gospel. Pray that every follower of Jesus would take seriously their responsibility to share the message of Christ.

- **Return Era:** God worked several miracles for His people through King Cyrus. Today, pray for your local government, including mayors, city council members, and others, and for the leaders of your state and country. Pray that God will accomplish His will through those who carry authority.

- **Silence Era:** All believers go through seasons when it feels as if God is silent. Discuss which passages of Scripture have helped you through such times. Also talk about when you have felt God's presence recently—perhaps while out in nature or during a time of worship at your church.

- **Poetical Books:** David was a masterful wordsmith, yet his best attribute was his love for God and desire to praise Him. Take a few minutes to write down some lines of praise to God. Think about an aspect of God that you admire—His power, compassion, love, justice, creativity, wisdom, and so on. If you feel comfortable, share your words with your partner.

- **Prophetical Books:** Discuss the difference you see between the prophets of the Old Testament predicting the future and people doing so today. Where can Christians find reliable "forthtelling" within the modern church?

FOR NEXT WEEK

Use the space below to write any insights or questions from your personal study that you want to discuss at the next group meeting. In preparation for next week, review chapters 15–19 in *30 Days to Understanding the Bible*.

THE HISTORY OF THE CHURCH

GOSPEL — MISSIONS ERAS

Humanity's link with God had been severed through sin.
But Jesus, as God incarnate, chose to accommodate us and a
provide a means for the relationship to be restored. His birth into
the world split history like a thunderbolt on a hot July evening.
His death on the cross in payment for our sin forever changed
history—for we now have the offer of eternal life with Him.

MAX ANDERS

WELCOME

Welcome to the fourth group session for *30 Days to Understanding the Bible*. For the past three weeks, we have explored the broad strokes of the Old Testament, including its geography, history, poetry, and prophets. Now it is time to transition into the New Testament.

However, before we move on, it is important to address a common misconception about the two parts of the Bible. Many who engage with Scripture come away believing—whether they articulate it or not—that the New Testament is more important than the Old Testament. Christians adopt this belief for many different reasons. The most notable is that the Old Testament feels more out of date with its focus on Israel, while the New Testament feels more current with its focus on Jesus and the launch of the church.

But let me say definitively that neither Testament of the Bible is more important than the other. As the apostle Paul wrote, "All Scripture is God-breathed and is useful for teaching, rebuking, correcting and training in righteousness" (2 Timothy 3:16). The Old Testament serves to reveal God through His laws and values and also through the nation of Israel. The New Testament is the history of another kind of revelation in the person of Jesus Christ, who is the fulfillment of God's law and a product of the nation of Israel.

Both halves are necessary to understand not only the Bible . . . but also God Himself.

SHARE

Jump into the theme of this session by discussing the following questions:

- When did you first hear about Jesus? How did you respond?

- Looking back at your notes, what stood out to you in your between-sessions studies that you would like to share with the group?

WATCH

Play the video segment for session four. As you watch, follow along with the main points listed in the outline below and record any key thoughts or concepts that stand out to you.

I. **Review:** Remember that by studying the "fourteeners" of the Bible, we are learning the basics of God's Word, not the whole. You should view this as the beginning of understanding the Bible, not the end.

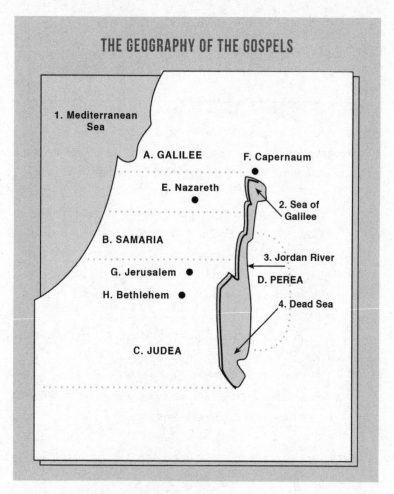

THE GEOGRAPHY OF THE GOSPELS

1. Mediterranean Sea
A. GALILEE
F. Capernaum
E. Nazareth
2. Sea of Galilee
B. SAMARIA
3. Jordan River
G. Jerusalem
D. PEREA
H. Bethlehem
4. Dead Sea
C. JUDEA

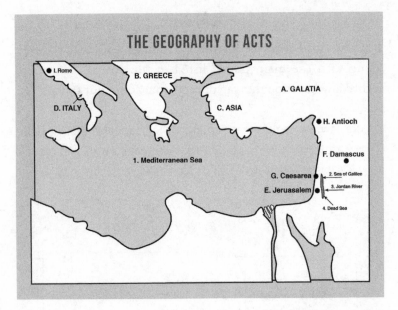

THE GEOGRAPHY OF ACTS

I.Rome • — D. ITALY — B. GREECE — A. GALATIA — C. ASIA — • H. Antioch — 1. Mediterranean Sea — F. Damascus • — G. Caesarea • — 2. Sea of Galilee — E. Jeruasalem • — 3. Jordan River — 4. Dead Sea

I. **Geography:** The geography of the New Testament is much more condensed than that of the Old Testament.

   A. The Old Testament takes place in an area roughly the size of Texas, while the Gospels are located primarily in an area smaller than New Hampshire.

   B. The "promised land" of Israel is small but has a remarkably varied landscape—including low deserts, high mountains, lush valleys, and more.

   C. There are four primary provinces (or regions) in the Gospels: Judea, Samaria, Galilee, and the Decapolis.

   D. The geography of the New Testament does expand in the book of Acts, where Paul's missionary journeys took him to modern-day Turkey, Greece, and Italy.

II. **Structure:** The overall structure of the New Testament is relatively simple.

A. There are five historical books: Matthew, Mark, Luke, John, and Acts.
B. The rest of the New Testament is a compilation of letters or "epistles," of which thirteen were written by Paul and nine were written by others.

NEW TESTAMENT BOOKS

Matthew	**To churches:**	Hebrews
Mark	Romans	James
Luke	1 Corinthians	1 Peter
John	2 Corinthians	2 Peter
Acts	Galatians	1 John
	Ephesians	2 John
	Philippians	3 John
	Colossians	Jude
	1 Thessalonians	Revelation
	2 Thessalonians	
	To individuals:	
	1 Timothy	
	2 Timothy	
	Titus	
	Philemon	

III. **History:** There are three historical eras in the New Testament.

    A. **The Gospel Era** tells the story of Jesus and includes these themes:

        1. His miraculous birth and early years, culminating in His baptism in the River Jordan.
        2. His early public ministry, which captured the attention of many people because of His miracles and other signs.
        3. His later ministry, which was marked by continued attack from continued attack and rejection from people who did not understand His message.
        4. His death and resurrection.

    B. **The Church Era** describes the initial birth and spread of the church, including:

        1. The birth of the church in Jerusalem.
        2. The organization of the church as numbers increased and a leadership structure became necessary.
        3. The persecution of the church as Jewish and Roman leaders took notice of this upstart band.
        4. The transition of the church expanding to include Gentiles.

    C. **The Missions Era** describes the spread of the church throughout the Roman Empire and beyond, including:

        1. In Paul's first missionary journey, he and Barnabas, his co-worker, traveled through modern-day Turkey on a church-planting mission.
        2. Paul's second missionary journey also included Turkey, but expanded into Macedonia (northern Greece) as well.

3. Pauls' third missionary journey included stops at his previous destinations, as well as further ventures.
4. Paul, Peter, and other church leaders suffered trials and imprisonment as a result of their missionary work.

IV. **The Epistles** of the New Testament were letters written by church leaders to address specific problems or encourage specific people within regional churches.

V. **Conclusion:** We have concluded the historical story of the Bible, but always remember that the Bible is more than a story.

A. The Bible also contains a set of teachings, or "doctrines," that help us understand God and the world around us.
B. In engaging these doctrines, it is important to pull together content from all areas of the Bible rather than simply focusing on a few specific pages.

DISCUSS

After watching the video, use the following questions to unpack what you learned as a group.

1. What is something new you learned during the teaching in this session? What is your greatest takeaway?

2. What are some similarities and differences between the content of the Old Testament and the New Testament?

_____

_____

_____

_____

_____

_____

_____

_____

3. What would you identify as the key elements of Jesus' story?

_____

_____

_____

_____

_____

_____

_____

4. The church has grown and expanded throughout history. How would you describe your experiences with individual churches and the church as a whole?

_____

_____

_____

_____

_____

_____

_____

5. The Missions Era of the church was critical to its survival. Where do you see opportunities for sharing the gospel in your community? Around the world?

_____

_____

_____

_____

_____

_____

6. What are you most excited about exploring or learning about the New Testament in the next few weeks? Why?

_____

_____

_____

_____

_____

_____

_____

APPLY

Prayer was a critical part of Jesus' ministry. He frequently went off alone to prayer, and on one occasion He even gave a "model prayer" to His disciples. Prayer was also a critical part of the church's initial launch. In the book of Acts, we read that Jesus' disciples gathered together to pray for forty days before the church officially launched on the Day of Pentecost. Prayer was also a key engine for the missionary activities of Paul, Barnabas, and others.

As you close this session, gather with your partner to spend some time in prayer. Begin by selecting a region of the world that you feel needs to better hear the gospel message. Spend time praying together for the people of that region, asking God to bring workers into the mission field and for opportunities to arise in your own lives for sharing God's Word.

BETWEEN-SESSIONS STUDY

Before you begin this personal study, make sure that you have reviewed chapters 15–19 in *30 Days to Understanding the Bible*. Be sure to also read the reflection questions after each activity and make a few notes in your guide about the experience. Once again, there will be a few minutes for you to share any insights you learned at the start of the next session.

DAY 16: GEOGRAPHY OF THE NEW TESTAMENT

If you get the chance to visit Israel, the guides and residents will often joke about how the nation's small size results in geographical landmarks gaining an exaggerated status. For example, any body of water that is too wide to swim across is a "sea," while every hill higher than your head is a "mountain." Knowing the locations and positions of these seas and mountains can help to create a mental picture of the events in the New Testament and help the story come alive. So, in beginning our exploration of the New Testament, we start with its geography.

BODIES OF WATER

Refer to the map of the geography in the Gospels in the group discussion section for this session. Notice there are four key bodies of water called out that you studied previously: (1) the Mediterranean Sea, (2) the Sea of Galilee, (3) the Jordan River, and

(4) the Dead Sea. Now refer to the map of the geography in the Book of Acts. Notice that the bodies of water are the same as for the Gospels—only much more of the Mediterranean Sea is involved.

As noted previously, the Sea of Galilee is only seven miles wide by fourteen miles long. The Dead Sea is ten miles by fifty miles, which is smaller than some nameless reservoirs in the United States. The Jordan River is little more than a strong-running creek compared to the truly mighty rivers of the world. But these bodies of water had tremendous importance in ancient times—especially to the residents of a desert climate such as Israel. So it is only fitting that several important moments in the New Testament occur in or near these bodies of water. And perhaps none is more significant than Jesus' baptism in the Jordan River.

> Then Jesus came from Galilee to the Jordan to be baptized by John. But John tried to deter him, saying, "I need to be baptized by you, and do you come to me?"
>
> Jesus replied, "Let it be so now; it is proper for us to do this to fulfill all righteousness." Then John consented.
>
> As soon as Jesus was baptized, he went up out of the water. At that moment heaven was opened, and he saw the Spirit of God descending like a dove and alighting on him. And a voice from heaven said, "This is my Son, whom I love; with him I am well pleased" (Matthew 3:13–17).

What evidence in the text suggests that this was an important moment in the history of the New Testament?

_____

_____

_____

_____

Why is it important to understand the geography of the nations, regions, and bodies of water described in the New Testament?

_____

_____

_____

_____

_____

_____

_____

LOCATIONS

There are eight key locations called out on the map of the geography in the Gospels: (A) Galilee (the province Jesus considered His home), (B) Samaria (a people of mixed race that lived in animosity with the Jews), (C) Judea (home to the city of Jerusalem), (D) Perea (a province on the east bank of the Jordan River), (E) Nazareth (where Jesus grew up), (F) Capernaum (the town that Jesus called home), (G) Jerusalem (the home of the temple, center of Jewish religious activity, and place of Jesus' death and resurrection), and (H) Bethlehem (Jesus' birthplace).

There are nine key locations called out on the map of the geography in the Book of Acts: (A) Galatia (the location of Paul's first missionary journey), (B) Greece (the location of Paul's second missionary journey), (C) Asia (the location of Paul's third missionary journey), (D) Italy (the location of Paul's final imprisonment), (E) Jerusalem (where the early church began), (F) Damascus (where Paul was headed when he met the risen Christ), (G) Caesarea (where Paul was put on trial), (H) Antioch (where Paul began his missionary journeys), and (I) Rome (the heart of the Roman Empire).

How can knowing the locations depicted in the Gospels help you to better understand where Jesus traveled and the obstacles that He might have faced?

_____

_____

_____

_____

How can knowing the locations depicted in the Book of Acts help you to better understand where Paul traveled and the obstacles that He might have faced?

_____

_____

_____

_____

_____

REVIEW

Fill in the blanks in each of the maps on the following page from memory. Note that the blanks with numbers are bodies of water, while the blanks with letters are locations.

DAY 17: THE GOSPEL ERA

The events in the Old Testament are grand in scope, covering a huge range of time and a wide array of peoples and nations. Genesis describes the creation of the world. Abraham walked the earth close to 2,000 years before Christ, and there were 1,000 years between Abraham and David. Jerusalem was destroyed in 587 BC, and the last of the prophets spoke several hundred years

THE GEOGRAPHY OF THE GOSPELS

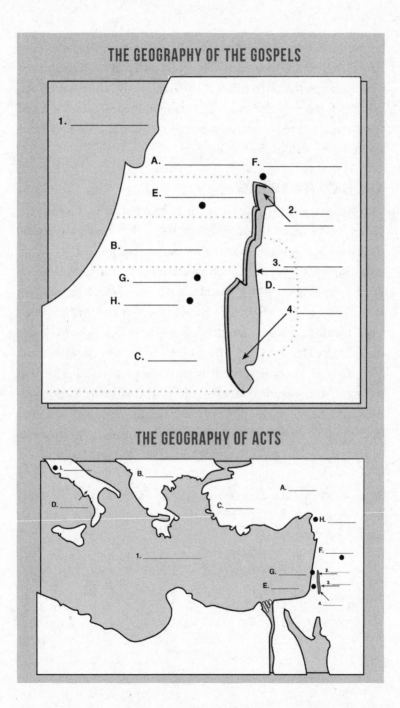

THE GEOGRAPHY OF ACTS

before Christ. In contrast, the events of the New Testament are condensed, as are the major characters and players. The span of time between the birth of John the Baptist and the final revelation from John the apostle is less than 100 years. Yet no span of years has been more consequential than those in which Jesus walked the earth in the Gospel Era.

JESUS' EARLY LIFE AND MINISTRY

The birth of Jesus in the city of Bethlehem, through a miraculous conception by the Holy Spirit, divided history as we know it. Everything before His birth we call BC (before Christ), while everything after we call AD. (*anno Domini*, or "in the year of our Lord"). Jesus grew up in the small town of Nazareth, and we know little of His life before His baptism in the Jordan River. This event, and Jesus' temptation in the wilderness for forty days, began His three-year ministry in Israel. During this time, He taught the people (primarily through parables), performed miracles, and demonstrated wisdom, compassion, righteousness, and justice in equal measures. Initially, Jesus was accepted by the people, but soon the Jewish religious leaders grew jealous of His popularity and influence and began to plot His death.

Jesus began His ministry by calling twelve men to follow Him and become His disciples. Why do you think Jesus chose to conduct His ministry in this manner?

_____

_____

_____

_____

_____

What is the significance of Jesus not only teaching the people great spiritual truths but also performing healings and miracles among them?

_____

_____

_____

_____

_____

_____

_____

_____

_____

DEATH AND RESURRECTION

Jesus began to call out the hypocritical attitudes of the Jewish religious leaders as the opposition mounted against Him. At the same time, He began to spend more time with His disciples, preparing them to carry on without Him. Eventually, Jesus is compelled to return to Jerusalem at the time of Passover to fulfill the mission that God has set for Him. Once there, the Jewish religious leaders stir up enthusiasm for Jesus' crucifixion, and the Roman governor reluctantly agrees to put Him to death on a cross. Jesus is taken down some time later and laid in a tomb. However, as the Gospel writers report, that is not the end of the story.

> After the Sabbath, at dawn on the first day of the week, Mary Magdalene and the other Mary went to look at the tomb.
>
> There was a violent earthquake, for an angel of the Lord came down from heaven and, going to the tomb, rolled back the stone and sat on it. His appearance was like lightning, and his clothes were white as snow. The

guards were so afraid of him that they shook and became like dead men.

The angel said to the women, "Do not be afraid, for I know that you are looking for Jesus, who was crucified. He is not here; he has risen, just as he said. Come and see the place where he lay. Then go quickly and tell his disciples: 'He has risen from the dead and is going ahead of you into Galilee. There you will see him.' Now I have told you."

So the women hurried away from the tomb, afraid yet filled with joy, and ran to tell his disciples. Suddenly Jesus met them. "Greetings," he said. They came to him, clasped his feet and worshiped him. Then Jesus said to them, "Do not be afraid. Go and tell my brothers to go to Galilee; there they will see me" (Matthew 28:1–10).

What are some of the key events of Jesus' resurrection as recorded in this passage?

_____

_____

_____

_____

_____

Why is this event so important in the lives of Christians today?

_____

_____

_____

_____

REVIEW

Write the correct number in the blank from the options on the right. (Refer to the notes you took in the "Watch" portion of this week's group study section if you need additional help.)

DIVISION	DESCRIPTION
Early Life:	1. Initial acceptance (Mark 1:21–28)
Early Ministry:	2. Final rejection (Matthew 26–28)
Later Ministry:	3. Childhood to baptism (Luke 2–3)
Death and Resurrection:	4. Growing rejection (John 6:60–71)

DAY 18: THE CHURCH ERA

People have different reactions to the idea of *church*. There are some who love the church experience. There are others who view the church as a necessary inconvenience. And there is a wide range of experiences in the middle. Yet while the church is certainly not perfect, it remains the instrument God chose to carry the message of the gospel to the world. In truth, any system that has people in it is going to be imperfect. But this is really the beauty of the church itself: it carries the gospel *to* imperfect people *by* imperfect people. Those imperfect people can then band together to help one another grow toward spiritual maturity.

THE BIRTH OF THE CHURCH

After Jesus' resurrection, He instructed His disciples to wait in the city of Jerusalem until they received the power of the Holy

Spirit. He told them that when they received this power, they would become witnesses for Christ in Jerusalem (which was their city), Judea and Samaria (which were the surrounding provinces), and the remotest parts of the earth. Following this, Jesus ascended into heaven right before their eyes. The disciples followed Jesus' instructions, and on the Day of Pentecost the Holy Spirit came upon them in such power that the world is still feeling the force of it.

> When the day of Pentecost came, they were all together in one place. Suddenly a sound like the blowing of a violent wind came from heaven and filled the whole house where they were sitting. They saw what seemed to be tongues of fire that separated and came to rest on each of them. All of them were filled with the Holy Spirit and began to speak in other tongues as the Spirit enabled them.
>
> Now there were staying in Jerusalem God-fearing Jews from every nation under heaven. When they heard this sound, a crowd came together in bewilderment, because each one heard their own language being spoken. Utterly amazed, they asked: "Aren't all these who are speaking Galileans? Then how is it that each of us hears them in our native language? Parthians, Medes and Elamites; residents of Mesopotamia, Judea and Cappadocia, Pontus and Asia, Phrygia and Pamphylia, Egypt and the parts of Libya near Cyrene; visitors from Rome (both Jews and converts to Judaism); Cretans and Arabs—we hear them declaring the wonders of God in our own tongues!" Amazed and perplexed, they asked one another, "What does this mean?" (Acts 2:1–12).

How did the coming of the Holy Spirit lead to many "God-fearing Jews" being exposed to the message of the gospel?

_____

_____

_____

_____

_____

Why is it critical for believers in the church today to continue reaching out to people from all nations and all people groups?

_____

_____

_____

_____

PERSECUTION AND TRANSITION

As the church begins to grow, the disciples decide to select a group of men (known as deacons) to look after the material needs of its poorer members. One of these deacons is a man named Stephen, who becomes the first Christian martyr after delivering a fiery sermon to the Jewish religious leaders, who quickly put him to death. This persecution spreads under the leadership of a man named Saul of Tarsus, and the believers are forced to flee to the surrounding regions. At one point Saul sets out to find a group of Christians who have fled to Samaria, but an encounter on the way forever changes the course of history.

> Saul was still breathing out murderous threats against the Lord's disciples. He went to the high priest and asked him for letters to the synagogues in Damascus, so that if he found any there who belonged to the Way, whether

men or women, he might take them as prisoners to Jerusalem. As he neared Damascus on his journey, suddenly a light from heaven flashed around him. He fell to the ground and heard a voice say to him, "Saul, Saul, why do you persecute me?"

"Who are you, Lord?" Saul asked.

"I am Jesus, whom you are persecuting," he replied. "Now get up and go into the city, and you will be told what you must do."

The men traveling with Saul stood there speechless; they heard the sound but did not see anyone. Saul got up from the ground, but when he opened his eyes he could see nothing. So they led him by the hand into Damascus. For three days he was blind, and did not eat or drink anything.

In Damascus there was a disciple named Ananias. The Lord called to him in a vision, "Ananias!"

"Yes, Lord," he answered.

The Lord told him, "Go to the house of Judas on Straight Street and ask for a man from Tarsus named Saul, for he is praying. In a vision he has seen a man named Ananias come and place his hands on him to restore his sight."

"Lord," Ananias answered, "I have heard many reports about this man and all the harm he has done to your holy people in Jerusalem. And he has come here with authority from the chief priests to arrest all who call on your name."

But the Lord said to Ananias, "Go! This man is my chosen instrument to proclaim my name to the Gentiles and their kings and to the people of Israel. I will show him how much he must suffer for my name" (Acts 9:1–16).

What did God say about Saul (whom we know as the apostle Paul) to Ananias? How did this signal a significant *transition* in the ministry of the early church?

_____

_____

_____

_____

_____

_____

What are some ways that believers in Christ are still persecuted today?

_____

_____

_____

_____

_____

REVIEW

Write the correct number in the blank from the options on the right. (Refer to the notes you took in the "Watch" portion of this week's group study section if you need additional help.)

DIVISION		DESCRIPTION
Birth:		1. A new leadership structure (Acts 6:1–7)
Organization:		2. Reaching the Gentiles (Acts 8:4–12:30)
Persecution:		3. Start of the church (Acts 2:1–47)
Transition:		4. Scattering of believers (Acts 6:8–8:3)

DAY 19: THE MISSIONS ERA

There are many things we take for granted in the modern world, but the ability to travel has to be near the top of the list. In most situations, anyone with the time and the means can transport themselves to the other end of the world in just a matter of hours! But in ancient times, Christians who wanted to spread the gospel around the known world committed themselves to extremely long voyages and years away from their friends and families.

PAUL'S MISSIONARY JOURNEYS

After Paul's conversion, he teamed up with several Christian brothers including Barnabas, Titus, Timothy, Mark, and others and traveled throughout the ancient world to share the gospel. The book of Acts describes three of Paul's missionary journeys to the regions of (1) Galatia, (2) Greece, and (3) Asia. Each of these journeys lasted for a period of several years, and each resulted in new churches being planted and cared for in the name of Christ. The following is just one example of what Paul endured on those journeys:

> The crowd joined in the attack against Paul and Silas, and the magistrates ordered them to be stripped and beaten with rods. After they had been severely flogged, they were thrown into prison, and the jailer was commanded to guard them carefully. When he received these orders, he put them in the inner cell and fastened their feet in the stocks.
>
> About midnight Paul and Silas were praying and singing hymns to God, and the other prisoners were listening to them. Suddenly there was such a violent earthquake that the foundations of the prison were shaken. At once all the prison doors flew open, and everyone's chains came loose. The jailer woke up, and when he saw the prison doors open, he drew his sword and was about to

kill himself because he thought the prisoners had escaped. But Paul shouted, "Don't harm yourself! We are all here!"

The jailer called for lights, rushed in and fell trembling before Paul and Silas. He then brought them out and asked, "Sirs, what must I do to be saved?"

They replied, "Believe in the Lord Jesus, and you will be saved—you and your household." Then they spoke the word of the Lord to him and to all the others in his house. At that hour of the night the jailer took them and washed their wounds; then immediately he and all his household were baptized. The jailer brought them into his house and set a meal before them; he was filled with joy because he had come to believe in God—he and his whole household (Acts 16:22–34).

What do you learn about Paul as a person from these verses?

_____

_____

_____

_____

_____

Throughout history, missionaries for the gospel have had to endure persecution and hardship of many kinds. Why might this be the case?

_____

_____

_____

_____

_____

PAUL'S TRIALS AND IMPRISONMENT

Eventually, the Jewish religious leaders in Jerusalem sought to have Paul arrested so they could put an end to his work of spreading the gospel. Paul is taken under guard to Caesarea, the Roman capital in the region, and tried under three leaders. At one point, Paul exercises his right as a Roman citizen to have his case heard before Caesar in Rome. The book of Acts ends with Paul under house arrest in Rome. Christian traditions relate that he was later beheaded, which was the established means of execution for a Roman citizen.

What do you think enabled Paul to remain faithful to his mission in the face of suffering?

What are some ways that you, your family, church, and/or denomination are currently contributing to the missions movement around the world?

REVIEW

Write the correct number in the blank from the options on the right. (Refer to the notes you took in the "Watch" portion of this week's group study section if you need additional help.)

SUBJECT	DESCRIPTION
First Missionary Journey:	1. House arrest in Rome (Acts 22–28)
Second Missionary Journey:	2. Ministry in Galatia (Acts 13–14)
Third Missionary Journey:	3. Ministry in Asia (Acts 18–21)
Trials and Imprisonment:	4. Ministry in Greece (Acts 15–17)

DAY 20: THE EPISTLES

Twenty years ago, people were bored with "snail mail" and excited to receive an e-mail from someone online. Now we are overloaded with electronic communications of all kinds—often to the point of exhaustion—and a handwritten letter is a welcome sight! Whatever the form, the purpose of such correspondence is always communication . . . and it was as necessary in the ancient world as it for us is today. For this reason, the early church leaders often composed lengthy letters to congregations that were in need of help to teach, encourage, correct, and inspire them.

PRINCIPLE AND PRACTICE

There are twenty-two such letters contained in the New Testament, which we refer to as the *epistles*. These letters were written to churches, individuals, and in some cases to the Christian public at large. They dealt with specific problems and issues of the day, but did so in a way that kept the information universal and timeless.

The typical pattern for a church leader drafting such an epistle was to first write a section of doctrinal truth and then follow it up with practical implications of that truth. In other words, the authors emphasized doctrine, then duty . . . principle, then practice. As an example, here is a beloved passage written by the apostle Paul to the Christians in Rome:

Love must be sincere. Hate what is evil; cling to what is good. Be devoted to one another in love. Honor one another above yourselves. Never be lacking in zeal, but keep your spiritual fervor, serving the Lord. Be joyful in hope, patient in affliction, faithful in prayer. Share with the Lord's people who are in need. Practice hospitality.

Bless those who persecute you; bless and do not curse. Rejoice with those who rejoice; mourn with those who mourn. Live in harmony with one another. Do not be proud, but be willing to associate with people of low position. Do not be conceited.

Do not repay anyone evil for evil. Be careful to do what is right in the eyes of everyone. If it is possible, as far as it depends on you, live at peace with everyone. Do not take revenge, my dear friends, but leave room for God's wrath, for it is written: "It is mine to avenge; I will repay," says the Lord. On the contrary:

"If your enemy is hungry, feed him;
    if he is thirsty, give him something to drink.
  In doing this, you will heap burning coals on
    his head."

Do not be overcome by evil, but overcome evil with good (Romans 12:9–21).

Where do you see elements of both *principle* and *practice* in these verses?

_____

_____

_____

_____

Why is it important for modern-day Christians to study letters written to churches that operated centuries ago?

_____

_____

_____

_____

_____

REVIEW

Write the correct number in the blank from the options on the right. (Refer to the "New Testament Books" chart in the "Watch" section if you need additional help.)

DISTINCTION		DESCRIPTION
Nature of the Epistles:		1. Letters to individuals and pastors
Paul's Epistles to Churches:		2. Letters to local churches
Paul's Epistles to Individuals:		3. Letters to the Christian public
General Epistles:		4. Doctrine, then duty

Fill in the blanks from memory:

ERA	SUMMARY
Creation:	Adam is created by God, but he _____. This is known as "the _____." This destroys God's original _____ for humans.
Patriarch:	Abraham is _____ by God to leave his own country and "father" a new _____.
Exodus:	Through Moses, the Hebrew people are _____ from slavery in the land of _____.
Conquest:	Joshua leads the _____ of the _____ _____.
Judges:	A group of leaders known as the _____ were chosen to _____ the Israelites for 400 rebellious years.
Kingdom:	David is the greatest king in the _____ Kingdom, but after his death there is a split between the Kingdom of _____ in the north and the Kingdom of _____ in the south.
Exile:	The rebellion of Judah and Israel leads to their _____ by outside powers and the _____ of the Jewish people.
Return:	God allows the captives to return to the city of _____, where they rebuild the temple, the city _____ under Nehemiah, and are reinstructed in God's _____ by leaders such as Ezra.
Silence:	During these years, the Jews organize into different political groups, including the _____ and the _____, and different religious groups, including the _____ and the _____.
Gospel:	Jesus enters the world as the promised Messiah, _____ the people through parables and performing _____. Many of the people _____ Him, leading to His death and _____.
Church:	The _____ is born on the Day of Pentecost. The believers soon endure _____ by the Jewish and Roman leaders.

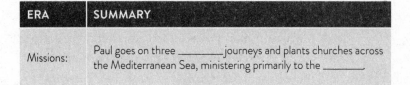

ERA	SUMMARY
Missions:	Paul goes on three _____ journeys and plants churches across the Mediterranean Sea, ministering primarily to the _____.

APPLY

Check in with your partner at least once this week to review what you studied. Use the following questions to help cement the main concepts in your minds

- **Patriarch Era:** Abraham's obedience resulted in the entire world being blessed. What is something God has recently commanded you to do? What is required of you to obey His call?

- **New Testament Geography:** Look at the map from this section. How might the people of Jesus' day navigated from place to place? What features of the landscape would have made traveling a challenge? If you were alive during Jesus' time, how much would you attempt to travel and "see the world"?

- **The Gospel Era:** Spend a few minutes together thanking Jesus for His sacrifice on the cross. Thank Him for His courage in accepting the weight of your sin. Praise Him for His faithfulness in taking the penalty. Praise Him for His power in defeating death and rising again so that you might be saved.

- **The Church Era:** Discuss some of the churches in your community. Talk about the possibility of visiting one of those churches as an educational opportunity. Is there a service you could attend together this week?

- **The Missions Era:** Check your church's website to identify which missionaries and/or missions organizations your church supports. Pray that more doors would be opened for sharing the gospel, planting churches, and making disciples. Also pray that God would provide every resource required for these missionaries and organizations to continue their work.

- **The Epistles:** Paul wrote, "Bless those who persecute you; bless and do not curse" (Romans 12:14). Discuss what it would look like to truly "bless" those who persecute you in a practical way. What steps can you take right now to put that blessing into practice?

FOR NEXT WEEK

Use the space below to write any insights or questions from your personal study that you want to discuss at the next group meeting. In preparation for next week, review chapters 20–25 in *30 Days to Understanding the Bible*.

THE GREAT DOCTRINES:

THE BIBLE, GOD, CHRIST, THE HOLY SPIRIT, AND ANGELS

The Bible is more than history. So, if we want to truly understand the Bible, we have to go beyond the historical study of people, places, and events and learn about its teachings. Taking the plunge is not easy, and it's difficult to get two people to agree on all points of doctrine. However, there is a basic body of doctrine on which all Christians historically have agreed.

MAX ANDERS

WELCOME

Welcome to the fifth group session for *30 Days to Understanding the Bible*. We have spent much of the past four weeks digging into the history of the Bible. But history is not the point of the Bible. Rather, history is only the vehicle through which God has revealed Himself through the pages of His Word.

In order to truly understand the Bible, we need to ask what it teaches us. What subjects does it cover? What does it say about each subject? When you add together the teachings of Moses, David, the prophets, Jesus, Paul, the apostles, and the rest, what did they teach about subjects such as God, man, angels, sin, salvation, angels, and the future? As we begin to answer these questions, we enter into the world of "biblical doctrine."

Now, the word *doctrine* may seem unsettling at first. Certainly, the church has squabbled for centuries over how different doctrines should be understood and which ones are most important. Even so, there is a body of doctrine on which nearly all Christians throughout the ages have agreed. So, during the final two weeks of this study, we will turn our focus to discussing these key doctrines. After all, understanding these biblical doctrines is a key element to understanding the Bible. So let's get to work!

SHARE

Jump into the theme of this session by discussing the following questions:

- What would you consider to be some of the essential doctrines of the Christian faith?

- Looking back at your notes, what stood out to you in your between-sessions studies that you would like to share with the group?

WATCH

Play the video segment for session five. As you watch, follow along with the main points listed in the outline below and record any key thoughts or concepts that stand out to you.

I. Knowledge is important for understanding the Bible.

   A. You can't believe something until you know it. You won't love something until you believe it.
   B. There are some truths so vital to the Christian life that you cannot fully follow God until you understand them.
   C. There are ten major doctrines in the Bible: the Bible, God, Christ, the Holy Spirit, Angels, Man, Sin, Salvation, the Church, and Future Things.

      1. All additional teachings in the Bible can fit under one or more of these ten key doctrines.
      2. As we explore these doctrines, we will look at a definition for each, an explanation for each, and central passages that reveal each to us.

II. **Doctrine of the Bible:** The Bible has a lot of say about the Bible, including:

   A. **Revelation:** The Bible was revealed to humankind by God.
   B. **Inspiration:** God saw to it that when people wrote down the words He that had revealed to them, they did so without error.
   C. **Illumination:** The Holy Spirit must enable people to understand and embrace the deeper truth of Scripture.
   D. **Interpretation:** We must be diligent students of the Bible to understand its deeper teachings.

III. **Doctrine of God:** The Bible teaches us the following about God:

    A. **Existence::** The reality of God lies outside of science's ability to prove, but the Bible addresses the topic head-on.

    B. **Attributes:** God exists as a person, and He has individual characteristics that are true of Him.

    C. **Sovereignty:** God is all-powerful and has the ability to do whatever He chooses.

    D. **Trinity:** God exists as one being in three distinct persons—the Father, the Son (Jesus), and Holy Spirit.

IV. **Doctrine of Christ:** There are four key elements to learning about Jesus:

    A. **Deity:** Jesus of Nazareth is God incarnate.

    B. **Humanity:** Jesus was also human—fully God and fully man.

    C. **Resurrection:** After being crucified, Jesus was raised to life again.

    D. **Return:** Jesus will return to earth as king at some point in the future.

V. **Doctrine of the Holy Spirit:** There are four major subdivisions to a biblical view of the Holy Spirit.

    A. **Personality:** The Holy Spirit is a personal being, not an impersonal force.

    B. **Deity:** The Spirit is divine—the third person of the Trinity.

    C. **Salvation:** The Spirit is instrumental to our personal salvation.

    D. **Gifts:** The Spirit imparts spiritual abilities to Christians.

VI. **Doctrine of Angels:** The Bible says the following about these heavenly beings:

A. **Angels**: The beings we know as these are ministering spirits from God.

B. **Demons:** These beings were formerly angels who served God but have fallen by choosing to rebel against God.

C. **Satan:** The highest of the demons; he began life as an angel but also rebelled against God and was expelled from heaven.

D. **Defenses:** Christians are able to use God's protection from evil through spiritual warfare.

VII. **Conclusion:** These ten major doctrines are critical for us to truly understand the Bible, and they build off one another.

A. These first five doctrines provide the spiritual foundation on which Christianity is built.

B. The next five doctrines will show how our everyday lives rest on that foundation.

C. Getting these essential truths in our minds and hearts is the beginning point for walking closer with God and living better in life.

DISCUSS

After watching the video, use the following questions to unpack what you learned as a group.

1. How would you describe your familiarity with biblical doctrines coming into this study?

2. Do you agree with the statement that you can't *believe* something until you know it and you won't *live* something until you believe it? Why or why not?

_____

_____

_____

_____

_____

_____

3. Why is it important to understand that Jesus was both fully divine and fully human?

_____

_____

_____

_____

_____

4. What are some ways you have experienced the Holy Spirit during your walk with God?

_____

_____

_____

_____

_____

_____

5. How would you summarize your understanding of angels, demons, and other spiritual beings? How would you summarize our society's understanding of these beings?

_____

_____

_____

_____

_____

6. Why is it critical for Christians to know and understand these doctrinal beliefs?

_____

_____

_____

_____

APPLY

During the teaching this week, you learned about a survey that painted a bleak picture of what Christians in America today understand about biblical doctrine. Learn more about that survey by searching for "The State of Theology" or by visiting thestateoftheology.com online. As you close this session, gather with your partner to read through the key findings of that survey, and then discuss the following questions: (1) What was the most surprising aspect of that survey? (2) How do you think you would have done if you were one of the Christians surveyed? (3) What are some practical steps that you could take today to increase your knowledge of biblical doctrine?

BETWEEN-SESSIONS STUDY

Before you begin this personal study, make sure that you have reviewed chapters 20-25 in *30 Days to Understanding the Bible*. Be sure to also read the reflection questions after each activity and make a few notes in your guide about the experience. Once again, there will be a few minutes for you to share any insights you learned at the start of the next session.

DAY 21: DOCTRINE OF THE BIBLE

A key component to understanding the Bible is gaining a working knowledge of what the Bible says about itself. Interestingly, the Bible does not defend itself. Nowhere in the Scriptures will you find a persuasive essay about why the Bible should be trusted. Instead, God's Word was written to people who accepted both its message and its authenticity. This being the case, the Bible offers an understanding of ultimate reality—telling us where we came from, where we are now, and where we are going. It is up to us to decide whether or not to accept the truth it offers.

REVELATION AND INSPIRATION

The fundamental assertion the Bible makes about itself is that—in spite of the fact that humans actually put its words on paper—it is a direct *revelation* of God to man, written without error, and can be trusted to reveal truth regarding God, humans, life, and death. In short, the Bible proclaims itself to be *inspired* by God. And when you look back at the impact this single volume has had on human history, there is little argument that can be made against that claim. The apostle Peter made the following compelling argument for the divine inspiration of the Bible:

> For we did not follow cleverly devised stories when we told you about the coming of our Lord Jesus Christ in power, but we were eyewitnesses of his majesty. He received honor and glory from God the Father when the voice came to him from the Majestic Glory, saying, "This is my Son, whom I love; with him I am well pleased." We ourselves heard this voice that came from heaven when we were with him on the sacred mountain.
>
> We also have the prophetic message as something completely reliable, and you will do well to pay attention to it, as to a light shining in a dark place, until the day dawns and the morning star rises in your hearts. Above all, you must understand that no prophecy of Scripture came about by the prophet's own interpretation of things. For prophecy never had its origin in the human will, but prophets, though human, spoke from God as they were carried along by the Holy Spirit (2 Peter 1:16–21).

How would you summarize Peter's argument for the divine origins of the Bible?

How have you come to trust the Bible in your own life?

_____

_____

_____

_____

_____

ILLUMINATION AND INTERPRETATION

Given the fact that the Bible is the revealed and inspired word of God, our natural ability to grasp and embrace the information it contains is limited. Much of what we read within its pages is spiritual and not readily easy for us to understand or accept. For this reason, the Holy Spirit works in our lives to *illuminate* our minds so we can comprehend and embrace its concepts. However, we still have a role to play in the process. For while it is true that we will never gain a deeper understand of the Bible without the work of the Holy Spirit, neither will we grasp the doctrines in the Bible unless we actively read it and study it. The more we seek to gain understanding of the Bible's truths, the more the Holy Spirit will illuminate those truths to us.

How have you personally seen the Holy Spirit illuminate passages of Scripture to you?

_____

_____

_____

_____

_____

What are some methods you have found effective in studying the Bible?

_____

_____

_____

_____

_____

_____

REVIEW

Look up the following passages and then indicate which of the topics it supports regarding the doctrine of the Bible: *revelation, inspiration, illumination,* or *interpretation.*

PASSAGES	TOPIC
1 Corinthians 2:12; Colossians 1:9:	
Hebrews 1:1; Hebrews 3:7:	
2 Timothy 2:15; Joshua 1:8:	
2 Peter 1:21; 2 Timothy 3:16:	

DAY 22: DOCTRINE OF GOD

Does God exist? Is there any such thing as God? Is God real? These are questions that have been asked, debated, and even fought over for thousands of years. Most of the time, in the vast majority of places, civilizations, and cultures, the answer has been, "Yes." For the most part, human beings seem to naturally conceive of and believe in the existence of the divine.

In modern society, we often get the impression that most "sophisticated" and truly educated people do not believe in God. However, this is an inaccurate claim. Yes, atheism has been on the rise in Western regions such as Europe and North America, but even so the overwhelming majority of people identify themselves as believers in some form or fashion of a divine being. In God. And there is good evidence for this belief.

THE EXISTENCE OF GOD

In our scientific-oriented culture, many people today are reluctant to believe in something they cannot *see, hear, smell, taste,* or *touch*. However, God cannot be dealt with in the laboratory. He must be dealt with in the courtroom. It is impossible to generate *proof* of His existence, so we must look for *evidence* of His existence. While the Bible simply assumes God exists, it also provides evidence to support that assumption, which means that believing in God's existence is an intellectually reasonable thing to do. In particular, the apostle Paul offers an excellent summary of that evidence in the following passage:

> The wrath of God is being revealed from heaven against all the godlessness and wickedness of people, who suppress the truth by their wickedness, since what may be known about God is plain to them, because God has made it plain to them. For since the creation of the world God's invisible qualities—his eternal power and divine nature—have been clearly seen, being understood from what has been made, so that people are without excuse.
>
> For although they knew God, they neither glorified him as God nor gave thanks to him, but their thinking became futile and their foolish hearts were darkened. Although they claimed to be wise, they became fools and

exchanged the glory of the immortal God for images made to look like a mortal human being and birds and animals and reptiles (Romans 1:18–23).

How would you summarize Paul's argument from these verses?

_____

_____

_____

_____

_____

Where do you find evidence in the natural world of God's "invisible qualities"?

_____

_____

_____

_____

THE ATTRIBUTES OF GOD

God is a personal being, and as such He has individual *characteristics* and *qualities* that distinguish Him from all other beings. Humankind shares some of these attributes, for all people were created in His image. We refer to these qualities as His "personal" attributes, and they include His *holiness, loving* nature, and His desire for *justice*. However, God also has other characteristics that go beyond human begins and are true of Him alone. We refer to these qualities as His "divine" attributes, and they include His *omnipotence* (God is all-powerful), His *omnipresence* (God is present everywhere), and His *omniscience* (God knows all things).

What are some ways that God has demonstrated His holiness and loving nature to you?

_____

_____

_____

_____

_____

When are some times that God demonstrated His power and presence to you?

_____

_____

_____

_____

_____

THE SOVEREIGNTY OF GOD

As we have seen, one of God's divine attributes is that He is omnipotent or all-powerful. This means that God has the sovereign ability to do whatever He wills on this earth, in our universe, and in our lives. God exercises His sovereignty in harmony with His goodness, holiness, and other attributes. Furthermore, the Bible tells us that God "does not change like shifting shadows" (James 1:17), which means God's sovereignty extends to the entirety of creation and for all time—both past, present, and future. The Bible reveals that God *alone* is sovereign—"the LORD is one" (Deuteronomy 6:4)—but a great mystery of Scripture is that He exists in *three* persons: Father, Son, and Holy Spirit. Historically, this concept is called the "Trinity."

What hope does it provide for you to know that God is sovereign over everything?

_____

_____

_____

_____

_____

What questions do you have about the *Trinity*—the fact that God is one but exists in three separate persons?

_____

_____

_____

_____

_____

REVIEW

Look up the following passages and then indicate which of the topics it supports regarding the doctrine of God: *existence, personal attributes, divine attributes, sovereignty,* or *Trinity.*

PASSAGES	TOPIC
Deuteronomy 6:4; 2 Corinthians 13:14:	
Job 42:2; Psalm 139:9; Psalm 139:4:	
Psalm 135:5–6; Psalm 115:3:	
Romans 1:20; Genesis 1:1:	
Isaiah 5:16; 1 John 4:8; Psalm 19:9:	

DAY 23: DOCTRINE OF CHRIST

There is perhaps no greater polarizing figure in history than Jesus Christ. In our culture today, Jesus is celebrated and followed by some ... but also ignored and disdained by others. The Christmas season is a powerful example. No other time of the year has such a broad impact on the culture (and the economy) than the one based on Jesus' birth. Yet for most people, the observance of that holiday has little to do with Christ. So, today, we will look at the identity of Jesus—who He was and how He came to have such an outsized influence on our world. Thankfully, the Bible provides ample information to guide us on these matters.

DEITY AND HUMANITY

One of the most difficult elements to grasp within the Bible's teachings about Jesus is that He is both fully God and fully human. Yet it is critical that we accept those dual aspects of Jesus' identity. Only because Jesus is fully God could He purchase forgiveness for sins through His death on the cross. But only because Jesus is fully human could He physically die. The apostle Paul wrote the following about this dual nature of Christ's identity:

> In your relationships with one another, have the same mindset as Christ Jesus:
>
> Who, being in very nature God,
>> did not consider equality with God something
>> to be used to his own advantage;
> rather, he made himself nothing
>> by taking the very nature of a servant,
>> being made in human likeness.
> And being found in appearance as a man,
>> he humbled himself

by becoming obedient to death—
even death on a cross!

Therefore God exalted him to the highest place
and gave him the name that is above every name,
that at the name of Jesus every knee should bow,
in heaven and on earth and under the earth,
and every tongue acknowledge that Jesus Christ is Lord,
to the glory of God the Father (Philippians 2:5–8).

What does Paul say about Jesus' humanity? What does he say about Jesus' divinity?

When did you first encounter Jesus in a real and meaningful way?

RESURRECTION AND RETURN

The Gospels reveal that Jesus was falsely accused by the Jewish religious leaders, tried, and ultimately handed over to the Romans to be executed. He was flogged—a punishment that killed sixty percent of its victims—before being forced to carry His own cross up to the place of His crucifixion. He experienced a physical death on that cross, and afterward was laid in a tomb owned by a man named Joseph of Arimathea. But after three days, Jesus rose from the dead, made numerous appearances to His disciples and followers, and then ascended into heaven after forty days. Jesus also promised that He would return again to this world—but this time not as a suffering servant but as a ruling king. These aspects of Jesus' identity were so central to the Christian faith that they became a form of "creed" in the early church:

> For what I received I passed on to you as of first importance: that Christ died for our sins according to the Scriptures, that he was buried, that he was raised on the third day according to the Scriptures, and that he appeared to Cephas, and then to the Twelve. After that, he appeared to more than five hundred of the brothers and sisters at the same time, most of whom are still living, though some have fallen asleep. Then he appeared to James, then to all the apostles, and last of all he appeared to me also, as to one abnormally born. . . .
>
> But Christ has indeed been raised from the dead, the firstfruits of those who have fallen asleep. For since death came through a man, the resurrection of the dead comes also through a man. For as in Adam all die, so in Christ all will be made alive. But each in turn: Christ, the firstfruits; then, when he comes, those who belong to him. Then the end will come, when he hands over the kingdom to God the Father after he has destroyed all dominion, authority and power. For he must reign until he has put all his enemies under his feet. The last enemy to be destroyed is death (1 Corinthians 15:3–8, 20–26).

How does Paul stress that Jesus physically died and rose again?

_____

_____

_____

_____

What does Paul say that Jesus will do when He returns to this world?

_____

_____

_____

REVIEW

Look up the following passages and then indicate which of the topics it supports regarding the doctrine of Christ: *deity, humanity, resurrection,* or *return.*

PASSAGES	TOPIC
Romans 1:4; John 11:25:	
John 1:14; Colossians 2:9:	
Titus 2:13; Matthew 25:31:	
John 1:1; John 17:5:	

DAY 24: DOCTRINE OF THE HOLY SPIRIT

The movie *Star Wars* has become a cultural landmark in our modern entertainment industry, generating billions of dollars in sales and spawning a series of sequels and prequels. One of the most memorable aspects of the movie franchise was the "the force," which was a mystical power within the *Star Wars* universe that influences characters, bestows certain powers, and is somehow connected to physical life. Unfortunately, many people today believe the Holy Spirit to be something similar to "the force." They think of God's Spirit as something that hovers within our world and carries an unknown influence within the church. Even when Christians talk about the Holy Spirit "living inside them," it is hard to articulate what that means.

PERSONALITY AND DEITY

So, just *who* is the Holy Spirit? Once again, the Bible reveals several important truths about the Holy Spirit to help us gain an understanding of His identity. Notice I said *His* identity—for the Bible reveals the Holy Spirit is not some form of ghost or floating spirit but an actual being. In Scripture, the Holy Spirit is treated like a *person*, with attributes of *emotions, actions,* and *intellect.* He is also depicted as a divine being—just as God and Jesus are divine—and possesses attributes such as omnipotence, omnipresence, and omniscience. Shortly before Jesus' death and resurrection, He said the following to His disciples about the Holy Spirit:

> "If you love me, keep my commands. And I will ask the Father, and he will give you another advocate to help you and be with you forever—the Spirit of truth. The world cannot accept him, because it neither sees him nor knows him. But you know him, for he lives with you and will be in you. . . .
>
> "All this I have spoken while still with you. But the Advocate, the Holy Spirit, whom the Father will send in my name, will teach you all things and will remind you of everything I have said to you. Peace I leave with you; my peace I give you. I do not give to you as the world

gives. Do not let your hearts be troubled and do not be afraid" (John 14:15–17, 25–27).

What are some ways the Holy Spirit works on our behalf?

How do you tend to perceive the Holy Spirit in your life?

SALVATION AND GIFTS

The Holy Spirit also plays an instrumental role in our personal salvation. He convicts us of our sin and helps us to see that we need to change our ways. He imparts a new spirit to us and allows us to experience eternal life with God in heaven. He dwells within us—just as God dwelt within the tabernacle and the temple in ancient Israel—and empowers us to grow more like Christ. He places us within the body of Christ and seals our relationship with God. Finally, the Holy Spirit gives us particular gifts that we are to use to further the work of the gospel and minister to others within the body of Christ. As Jesus again said about the Holy Spirit:

> "It is for your good that I am going away. Unless I go away, the Advocate will not come to you; but if I go, I will send him to you. When he comes, he will prove the world

to be in the wrong about sin and righteousness and judgment: about sin, because people do not believe in me; about righteousness, because I am going to the Father, where you can see me no longer; and about judgment, because the prince of this world now stands condemned.

"I have much more to say to you, more than you can now bear. But when he, the Spirit of truth, comes, he will guide you into all the truth. He will not speak on his own; he will speak only what he hears, and he will tell you what is yet to come. He will glorify me because it is from me that he will receive what he will make known to you. All that belongs to the Father is mine. That is why I said the Spirit will receive from me what he will make known to you" (John 16:7–15).

What does Jesus say that the Holy Spirit does as it relates to convicting people of sin?

_____

_____

_____

_____

_____

In what ways have you experienced the Holy Spirit's convicting work in your own life?

_____

_____

_____

_____

REVIEW

Look up the following passages and then indicate which of the topics it supports regarding the doctrine of the Holy Spirit: *personality, deity, salvation,* or *gifts.*

PASSAGES	TOPIC
1 Corinthians 12:4, 11; 1 Peter 4:10:	
2 Corinthians 13:14; John 15:26:	
John 16:8; Titus 3:5; Romans 8:9:	
Ephesians 4:30; Isaiah 63:10:	

DAY 25: DOCTRINE OF ANGELS

It's a common trope of movies and TV shows. Viewers are shown a character who has an important decision to make. Perhaps the person is being tempted to commit an evil act. All of a sudden, a little angel pops up on the character's right shoulder and advises to do the right thing. The next moment, a red devil with horns and a pitchfork shows up on the other shoulder, giving the opposite advice. Sadly, angels are given little respect in our culture. In fact, Christians who declare their belief in the existence of angels (or demons) are often ridiculed as uneducated or unrefined. This has not been the case for the vast majority of human history.

ANGELS AND DEMONS

The Bible teaches that God uses an army of angels to help execute His will in heaven and earth, and that among their duties is ministering to Christians. These angels are personal beings—spirits God created before Adam and Eve. A number of these angels rebelled against God, and they now form an army under the command of Satan. We call these evil spirits *demons*, and, like angels, they carry a real influence in our world. The conflict between the spiritual forces of good and evil is often called "spiritual warfare," and all humans who follow Christ are called to participate in the fight. Paul pulled back the veil on this spiritual conflict when he wrote:

> Finally, be strong in the Lord and in his mighty power. Put on the full armor of God, so that you can take your stand against the devil's schemes. For our struggle is not against flesh and blood, but against the rulers, against the authorities, against the powers of this dark world and against the spiritual forces of evil in the heavenly realms. Therefore put on the full armor of God, so that when the day of evil comes, you may be able to stand your ground, and after you have done everything, to stand. Stand firm then, with the belt of truth buckled around your waist, with the breastplate of righteousness in place, and with your feet fitted with the readiness that comes from the gospel of peace. In addition to all this, take up the shield of faith, with which you can extinguish all the flaming arrows of the evil one. Take the helmet of salvation and the sword of the Spirit, which is the word of God (Ephesians 6:10–17).

How have you experienced the "struggle" Paul described?

_____

_____

_____

_____

_____

What are some appropriate ways to discuss angels, demons, and other spiritual realities with those who are not followers of Jesus?

_____

_____

_____

_____

SATAN AND DEFENSES

The Bible teaches that Satan was originally the highest angel, but because of his pride, he rebelled against the Lord and led a number of other angels to rebel as well. In doing this, he became evil and corrupt. Satan is thus a real being who oversees the forces of darkness in this world. Jesus accurately described his character when He said, "He was a murderer from the beginning, not holding to the truth, for there is no truth in him. When he lies, he speaks his native language, for he is a liar and the father of lies" (John 8:44). Fortunately, as we saw in the previous passage, God has given us many spiritual defenses to withstand Satan's attacks. The prophet Isaiah is believed to have been writing about the fall of Satan when he wrote:

> How you have fallen from heaven,
>   morning star, son of the dawn!
> You have been cast down to the earth,
>   you who once laid low the nations!
> You said in your heart,
>   "I will ascend to the heavens;
> I will raise my throne
>   above the stars of God;
> I will sit enthroned on the mount of assembly,
>   on the utmost heights of Mount Zaphon.

I will ascend above the tops of the clouds;
    I will make myself like the Most High."
But you are brought down to the realm of the dead,
    to the depths of the pit (Isaiah 14:12–15).

Why do you think people try to deny the existence of Satan and demons today?

_____

_____

_____

_____

What are some the ways that God has helped you to withstand Satan's attacks?

_____

_____

_____

REVIEW

Look up the following passages and then indicate which of the topics it supports regarding the doctrine of angels: *angels, demons, Satan,* or *defenses.*

PASSAGES	TOPIC
Hebrews 1:14; Psalm 91:11:	
1 Peter 5:8; John 8:44:	
2 Corinthians 2:11; Ephesians 6:13:	
Jude 1:6; 2 Peter 2:4:	

Fill in the blanks from memory:

DOCTRINE	SUMMARY
The Bible:	The Bible was _____ to humans by God. God _____ the words that were written. The Holy Spirit _____ the Bible so we can understand it. We must be diligent to _____ its teachings.
God:	God has _____ in the past and will _____ in the future. The Bible teaches _____ about His nature, one of which is that God is _____ over all creation. God exists in what we call the _____, consisting of the Father, Son, and Holy Spirit.
Christ:	Jesus was God-incarnate or _____, yet He was also fully _____ like us. After His death for our sin, He was _____ from the dead. He will one day _____ as a conquering king.
Holy Spirit:	The Holy Spirit is a _____ like God the Father and Jesus the Son and is fully _____ as well. He is instrumental in our _____, by which we receive God's forgiveness and experience eternal life. He also provides _____ for us to use to serve in the church.
Angels:	_____ are ministering spirits from God, while _____ are angels who _____ against God. _____ is the highest angel who fell. God has given us _____ to guard against his attacks.

APPLY

Check in with your partner at least once this week to review what you studied. Use the following questions to help cement the main concepts in your minds.

- **Doctrine of the Bible:** Find any unused Bibles in your home and gather them together. Pray with your partner for God to give you an opportunity to share one or more of those Bibles with others who may need them—and especially with those who have little or no experience with God's Word.

- **Doctrine of God:** David wrote, "The heavens declare the glory of God" (Psalm 19:1). This week, work out a way for you and your partner to spend some time together in nature. Talk with each other about the evidence for God's existence that is apparent in what you find.

- **Doctrine of Christ:** Talk with your partner about several verses in the Bible that are especially meaningful to you regarding the character and nature of Christ. Commit to memorizing one or two of these verses this week.

- **Doctrine of the Holy Spirit:** Check in with your partner to talk through the implications of the Holy Spirit's existence as a relatable person. How does the Spirit's "personhood" impact your communication with Him through prayer? How does it influence your approach to worship? How does it influence your approach to spiritual warfare?

- **Doctrine of Angels:** Pray together that God would equip you with His spiritual armor. Pray to be equipped with each piece of armor specifically—the belt of truth, the breastplate of righteousness, the shoes of the gospel of peace, the helmet of salvation, and the sword of the Spirit.

FOR NEXT WEEK

Use the space below to write any insights or questions from your personal study that you want to discuss at the next group meeting. In preparation for next week, review chapters 26–30 in *30 Days to Understanding the Bible*.

THE GREAT DOCTRINES:

MAN, SIN, SALVATION, THE CHURCH, AND FUTURE THINGS

An old Irish prayer says, "O Lord, turn the hearts of our enemies.
And if You can't turn their hearts, then turn their ankles,
so we can know them by their limp." There are many people limping,
in the eyes of others, over certain doctrinal distinctions.
But as we have seen, there are several key doctrines in the Bible
on which we all can agree—and all need to know.

MAX ANDERS

WELCOME

Welcome to the final group session for *30 Days to Understanding the Bible*! Last week, we started our journey of understanding not only the overarching *story* of the Bible but also what the Bible *teaches* by looking at the doctrines of the Bible, God, Christ, the Holy Spirit, and angels. This week, we will continue our exploration by focusing on five more key doctrines, including the doctrines of *man, sin, salvation,* the *church,* and *future things.*

As I mentioned at the beginning of this study, the Bible is an enormous book covering a vast amount of information, eras, and subjects. No matter h w studious a person you are, it is simply not possible to learn everything about it over the course of a six-week study. However, it is my hope that as you have gone through the material and done all of the exercises, that you now have a greater understanding of the "fourteeners" of God's Word—those high points and crucial events in Scripture that provide the key to understanding the Bible as a whole.

As we conclude this study, I encourage you to take four steps to continue the journey: (1) read the Bible, (2) study the Bible, (3) memorize the Bible, and (4) meditate on the Bible. These steps seem simple enough, but the trick is taking them all. Some people just take the first step of reading the Bible but then fail to study it, memorize it, or meditate on it. As a result, they do not experience the full life of spiritual transformation that God desires them to have. Don't let this be true of you! Continue to take these steps on the path of understanding.

As you commit to doing this, *you will begin to master the Bible so well that the Bible begins to master you.* And as the Bible begins to master you, you will enjoy the inner peace, love, and joy that is the fruit of the Holy Spirit. In addition, you will experience a peace and power in life and ministry that the Holy Spirit gives to those who meditate on God's Word. So, with this in

mind . . . let's dive into our exploration of the final five key
doctrines of the Bible.

SHARE

Jump into the theme of this session by discussing the following
questions:

- What surprised you the most in your study of the five
  biblical doctrines we covered—the Bible, God, Christ,
  the Holy Spirit, and angels?

- Looking back at your notes, what stood out to you in
  your between-sessions studies that you would like to
  share with the group?

WATCH

Play the video segment for session six. As you watch, follow
along with the main points listed in the outline below and
record any key thoughts or concepts that stand out to you.

I. Remember that our journey toward understanding the Bible
    has been a "big picture" approach.

    A. We've explored the big picture of the Bible's structure.
    B. We've explored the big picture of biblical history in the Old
       and New Testaments.
    C. We've explored the big picture of the Bible's poetry, proph-
       ets, and epistles.
    D. We've started gaining a big picture of Bible doctrines, and
       we will finish that picture this week.

II. **Doctrine of Man:** The Bible offers an understanding of humanity (male and female) in four parts.

    A. **Origin:** Humans were created by God in His image.

    B. **Nature:** People have a spiritual and as a physical dimension.

    C. **Distinctiveness:** Man has capabilities that go beyond those of animals and mark us as the pinnacle of God's creation.

    D. **Destiny:** Humans will live forever in either heaven or in hell.

III. **Doctrine of Sin:** What the Bible says fits into four themes.

    A. **Nature:** Sin is lack of conformity to God's moral perfection.

    B. **Fall:** The moment of separation of Adam and Eve from God in the Garden of Eden because they disobeyed His instructions.

    C. **Corruption:** Humanity as a whole was corrupted by the fall.

    D. **Rebellion:** Because our internal nature has been corrupted by sin, we cannot keep from committing personal sins.

IV. **Doctrine of Salvation:** Let's look at four major subdivisions.

    A. **Basis:** Salvation is a gift God gives to those who believe.

    B. **Result:** God extends forgiveness and eternal life to those who accept Him.

    C. **Cost:** The penalty of sin is paid for by the substitutionary death of Christ.

    D. **Timing:** Our salvation is completed at the death of the body.

V. **Doctrine of the Church:** There are four themes here as well.

    A. **Universal Church:** The totality of all believers in Jesus.

    B. **Local Church:** A local group of believers organized to carry out the ideas of the universal church.

C. **Church Leadership:** Leaders are those in the church worthy of being followed because of their spiritual gifts and spiritual maturity.

D. **Church Membership:** Belonging to the universal church and a local church.

VI. **Doctrine of Future Things:** There is a wide range of beliefs about biblical prophecy, but all agree upon four main subdivisions of this doctrine.

A. **Return:** Jesus will return to earth again at a future time.

B. **Judgment:** God will confirm the eternal destiny of all people.

C. **Universe:** The old order will be destroyed and replaced with a new one.

D. **Eternity:** Christians will live with God forever.

VII. **Conclusion:** You have completed *30 Days to Understanding the Bible*. Well done! Remember we have only reviewed the "fourteeners" of the Bible. There is still much more to be learned!

DISCUSS

After watching the video, use the following questions to unpack what you learned as a group.

1. Of the five doctrines mentioned during the teaching this, which do you feel most confident discussing? Why?

_____

_____

_____

_____

2. What are some similarities and differences between the Bible's view of humanity and society's view?

_____

_____

_____

_____

_____

_____

_____

3. Why is sin something we need to talk about both in the church and in our culture?

_____

_____

_____

_____

_____

_____

_____

4. How would you explain the idea of salvation to someone who has never heard it?

_____

_____

_____

_____

_____

_____

_____

5. Do you feel that church membership and church attendance are necessary for Christians? Why or why not?

    _____

    _____

    _____

    _____

    _____

    _____

6. The doctrine of future things is controversial within the church. How much time should Christians spend attempting to figure out the future?

    _____

    _____

    _____

    _____

    _____

    _____

APPLY

All cave explorers know to bring along a source of light when they go spelunking. Caves are so dark that without some form of light—even if just a flicker—they would never be able find their way back to the entrance. For this reason, responsible spelunkers take several helmet lights, handheld flashlights, and a fistful of spare batteries. Light makes all the difference.

As one psalmist declared, "Your word is a lamp for my feet, a light on my path" (Psalm 119:105). The metaphor is clear. If we do not know the Word of God, or if we have not mastered the Bible to the point that it penetrates our hearts, controls our beliefs, and ultimately changes our actions and behaviors, we are groping in the darkness like a spelunker without a flashlight. We will stumble into danger, wander in circles, and pass by avenues of escape.

As you close this session, get with your partner and identify a Bible-reading plan that each of you can follow for the next several months . . . or even an entire year. Commit to exploring God's Word each day through study, memorization, and meditation on specific passages. Be sure to also talk regularly about what you've read and what you've learned.

BETWEEN-SESSIONS STUDY

Before you begin this personal study, make sure that you have reviewed chapters 26–30 in *30 Days to Understanding the Bible*. Be sure to also read the reflection questions after each activity and make a few notes in your guide about the experience. Share these insights with your partner in the days and weeks following the conclusion of this study.

DAY 26: DOCTRINE OF MAN

There is no doubt that God is the central player in the Bible. Throughout the biblical text, it is God who creates, God who plans, God who calls, and God who redeems. The Bible is God's story from beginning to end. Yet the Bible is also the story of humanity. It is the story of God creating humanity, God planning for the needs of humanity, God calling servants and prophets to proclaim His will to humanity, and ultimately God redeeming humanity. In other words, the Bible is God's story, yet the primary focus of that story is God's love for humanity—the pinnacle of His creation—and His desire for a relationship with us.

ORIGIN AND NATURE

There are many areas in which the teachings of the Bible clash with the conclusions generated by science. But one of the greatest clashes addresses the nature of human beings at the core. According to a purely scientific way of thinking, people developed through a process of evolution and are only physical beings. In contrast, the Bible teaches that we were created by God and that we are spiritual as well as physical. Our physical body is destined to die, but our spirit is destined to live forever and transcend our physical limitations. As Paul wrote:

> If there is a natural body, there is also a spiritual body. So it is written: "The first man Adam became a living being"; the last Adam, a life-giving spirit. The spiritual did not come first, but the natural, and after that the spiritual. The first man was of the dust of the earth; the second man is of heaven. As was the earthly man, so are those who are of the earth; and as is the heavenly man, so also are those who are of heaven. And just as we have borne the image of the earthly man, so shall we bear the image of the heavenly man.
>
> I declare to you, brothers and sisters, that flesh and blood cannot inherit the kingdom of God, nor does the perishable inherit the imperishable. Listen, I tell you a mystery: We will not all sleep, but we will all be changed—in a flash, in the twinkling of an eye, at the last trumpet. For the trumpet will sound, the dead will be raised imperishable, and we will be changed. For the perishable must clothe itself with the imperishable, and the mortal with immortality. When the perishable has been clothed with the imperishable, and the mortal with immortality, then the saying that is written will come true: "Death has been swallowed up in victory" (1 Corinthians 15:44–54).

Why is it important to understand that humans were created by God in His image?

_____

_____

_____

_____

Why is understanding the dual nature of humankind important for understanding the broader teachings of the Bible?

_____

_____

_____

_____

DISTINCTIVENESS AND DESTINY

Human beings possess intellect, emotions, and will. Our intellect allows us to know, reason, and think. Our emotions enable us to feel, empathize, and experience. Our will allows us to make choices. We also have the capacity for self-awareness, an awareness of God, an awareness of the afterlife, and the ability to envision life in the future. We have many characteristics that overlap with the animal kingdom—but we are *distinct* in that we have abilities and capacities that no other creature on earth possesses. Furthermore, the Bible reveals that we all have an eternal *destiny*. Jesus spoke about the destiny that awaited His followers:

> "Do not let your hearts be troubled. You believe in God; believe also in me. My Father's house has many rooms; if that were not so, would I have told you that I am going there to prepare a place for you? And if I go and prepare a place for you, I will come back and take you to be with

me that you also may be where I am. You know the way to the place where I am going" (John 14:1–4).

What promises does Jesus make to His followers in this passage?

_____

_____

_____

_____

_____

_____

How does it make you feel to know that you were created by God in His own image?

_____

_____

_____

_____

_____

REVIEW

Look up the following passages and then indicate which of the topics it supports regarding the doctrine of man: *origin, nature, distinctiveness,* or *destiny.*

PASSAGES	TOPIC
Genesis 1:26; Ephesians 2:10:	
Hebrews 9:27; John 3:16:	
Genesis 1:27; Genesis 9:6:	
1 Thessalonians 5:23; 2 Peter 1:4:	

DAY 27: DOCTRINE OF SIN

If there is one word that makes people most uncomfortable in a church setting, that word might be *sin*. To put it bluntly, we don't like talking about sin. We don't like thinking about sin. And we definitely don't like being told that we need to deal with our sin. Yet the Bible is clear that we *do* need to deal with our transgressions before God. There are two reasons for this. First, sin is harmful to us—it is self-destructive. All sins are like boomerangs that come back to hurt us every time. Second, sin separates us from God. If we hope to live a life in fellowship with Him, it means accepting the challenge of growing in righteousness.

NATURE AND FALL

To understand the doctrine of sin, we first need to have a working definition of sin. In the Hebrew language of the Old Testament, the word *sin* carried the idea of "missing the mark," much like an archer missing the target. So, we can define *sin* as *any lack of conformity to the mark that God has set for moral perfection.* As we have learned in this study, sin entered the world when Adam and Eve disobeyed God in the Garden of Eden—what we call the "fall." All the pain, suffering, and evil in this world can be traced back to that one event.

> Then the man and his wife heard the sound of the Lord God as he was walking in the garden in the cool of the day, and they hid from the Lord God among the trees of the garden. But the Lord God called to the man, "Where are you?"
>
> He answered, "I heard you in the garden, and I was afraid because I was naked; so I hid."
>
> And he said, "Who told you that you were naked? Have you eaten from the tree that I commanded you not to eat from?" . . .

To the woman he said,

"I will make your pains in childbearing very severe;
    with painful labor you will give birth to children.
Your desire will be for your husband,
    and he will rule over you."

To Adam he said, "Because you listened to your wife and ate fruit from the tree about which I commanded you, 'You must not eat from it,'

"Cursed is the ground because of you;
    through painful toil you will eat food from it
    all the days of your life.
It will produce thorns and thistles for you,
    and you will eat the plants of the field.
By the sweat of your brow
    you will eat your food
until you return to the ground,
    since from it you were taken;
for dust you are
    and to dust you will return" (Genesis 3:8–11, 16–19).

What was Adam and Eve's reaction when they heard God? In what ways is this still a common response to the Lord when we realize we have sinned?

What were some of the consequences for Adam and Eve's sin against God?

_____

_____

_____

_____

_____

CORRUPTION AND REBELLION

By nature, ever since the time of the fall, we have been creatures who sin. It is not that we are incapable of doing good. Rather, because of sin, we cannot keep from doing wrong because our essential nature has been *corrupted*. We are not sinners because we sin . . . we sin because we are sinners. Some of these sins are sins of commission (things we should not do but do) and some are sins of omission (things we should do but do not). In a sense, we are in a state of rebellion against God. Paul lamented about our sinful nature when he wrote:

> We know that the law is spiritual; but I am unspiritual, sold as a slave to sin. I do not understand what I do. For what I want to do I do not do, but what I hate I do. And if I do what I do not want to do, I agree that the law is good. As it is, it is no longer I myself who do it, but it is sin living in me. For I know that good itself does not dwell in me, that is, in my sinful nature. For I have the desire to do what is good, but I cannot carry it out. For I do not do the good I want to do, but the evil I do not want to do—this I keep on doing. Now if I do what I do not want to do, it is no longer I who do it, but it is sin living in me that does it.

So I find this law at work: Although I want to do good, evil is right there with me. For in my inner being I delight in God's law; but I see another law at work in me, waging war against the law of my mind and making me a prisoner of the law of sin at work within me. What a wretched man I am! Who will rescue me from this body that is subject to death? Thanks be to God, who delivers me through Jesus Christ our Lord! (Romans 7:14–25).

Paul expressed his frustration with the way sin corrupted his thoughts and actions. When have you felt the same way?

_____

_____

_____

_____

_____

_____

_____

What are some appropriate ways to talk about sin with others in the church?

_____

_____

_____

_____

_____

_____

_____

_____

REVIEW

Look up the following passages and then indicate which of the topics it supports regarding the doctrine of sin: *nature, fall, corruption,* or *rebellion.*

PASSAGES	TOPIC
1 John 5:17; Mark 7:20–23:	
Romans 3:23; Romans 6:23:	
Ephesians 2:1, 3; Psalm 51:5:	
Genesis 3:6; Romans 5:12:	

DAY 28: DOCTRINE OF SALVATION

Do you remember a major turning point in your life? All of us have them—instances when we make a decision or are part of an event that changed the course of our entire lives. It may be a decision to attend a certain school or marry your spouse. It could be a medical diagnosis. It could be the birth of a child or the death of a loved one. For Christians, there is no greater turning point than the moment of our salvation. Before this moment, we were spiritually dead because of sin. But then, because of the gift of redemption offered by Jesus on the cross, we were made alive and transformed into something entirely new: *a child of God.*

BASIS AND RESULT

The Bible is clear that salvation cannot be earned. As humans born into a corrupted world, we are imperfect and have no way of making ourselves perfect. However, God is perfect, and He demands perfection of all who would enter His kingdom. So, in His mercy, the Lord provided a way for us to be saved through the death and resurrection of Jesus. He offers us *forgiveness* for our sins and gives us a new nature that is not flawed by sin. Our part in the process is to accept God's gift of salvation and embrace this new nature that He has given to us.

> As for you, you were dead in your transgressions and sins, in which you used to live when you followed the ways of this world and of the ruler of the kingdom of the air, the spirit who is now at work in those who are disobedient. All of us also lived among them at one time, gratifying the cravings of our flesh and following its desires and thoughts. Like the rest, we were by nature deserving of wrath. But because of his great love for us, God, who is rich in mercy, made us alive with Christ even when we were dead in transgressions—it is by grace you have been saved. And God raised us up with Christ and seated us with him in the heavenly realms in Christ Jesus, in order that in the coming ages he might show the incomparable riches of his grace, expressed in his kindness to us in Christ Jesus. For it is by grace you have been saved, through faith—and this is not from yourselves, it is the gift of God—not by works, so that no one can boast. For we are God's handiwork, created in Christ Jesus to do good works, which God prepared in advance for us to do (Ephesians 2:1–10).

What do you remember about your earliest encounters with the idea of salvation?

_____

_____

_____

_____

What are the most significant ways your life has changed since the moment of your salvation?

_____

_____

_____

_____

COST AND TIMING

The Bible reveals the penalty for sin is *death*. Only Jesus could pay the cost for our sin because only He lived a completely sinless life. His death on the cross thus served as a substitution for our own death. God counts Jesus' death for our own and grants us eternal life when we accept His gift of salvation and embrace our new nature. Of course, it would be wonderful at this point if we no longer experienced the pull of temptation or the effects of sin. But the truth is that our minds remain corrupted with old programming that is counter to biblical truth. This results in a continual struggle between our born-again inner nature that wants to serve God and our outer nature that is still pulled toward sin. This conflict continues until the death of our physical body, at which point we are transported to heaven to receive a new body untouched by sin.

> I consider that our present sufferings are not worth comparing with the glory that will be revealed in us. For the creation waits in eager expectation for the children of God to be revealed. For the creation was subjected to frustration, not by its own choice, but by the will of the one who subjected it, in hope that the creation itself will be liberated from its bondage to decay and brought into the freedom and glory of the children of God.

We know that the whole creation has been groaning as in the pains of childbirth right up to the present time. Not only so, but we ourselves, who have the firstfruits of the Spirit, groan inwardly as we wait eagerly for our adoption to sonship, the redemption of our bodies. For in this hope we were saved. But hope that is seen is no hope at all. Who hopes for what they already have? But if we hope for what we do not yet have, we wait for it patiently (Romans 8:18–25).

How did the apostle Paul view his present sufferings in this world?

_____

_____

_____

_____

_____

_____

_____

What future hope did he possess that enabled him to take this attitude?

_____

_____

_____

_____

_____

_____

_____

REVIEW

Look up the following passages and then indicate which of the topics it supports regarding the doctrine of salvation: *basis, result, cost,* or *timing.*

PASSAGES	TOPIC
1 Peter 3:18; Hebrews 9:12:	
Romans 8:23; John 11:25–26:	
Ephesians 2:8–9; Titus 2:11:	
1 John 1:9; Romans 10:9:	

DAY 29: DOCTRINE OF THE CHURCH

The church does not always receive respect these days. In fact, it is often mocked and ridiculed. Some of that ridicule has been earned because of scandals and hypocrisy among its members. Those who expect church leaders and members to be perfect will always be disappointed. Even so, we need to remember God's original purpose and intention for the church—and recognize that it is the method He has chosen to spread the gospel. Given this, it is time for us to regard the church as God regards it—and to also love the church as He loves it.

UNIVERSAL AND LOCAL

People often confuse the idea of "church" with the church buildings they see out in the world. The truth is that the church is much more than a building or even a collection of buildings. The church is the *universal* gathering of all who follow Christ in every corner of the world—past, present, and future. In the Bible, the church is often referred to as the "body of Christ," and in many ways it functions that way—with each member contributing to the whole. Yet the church is also *local*, in that it operates in communities where people live and work. Thus, Christians in the local church band together to carry out the responsibilities of the universal church.

As you come to him, the living Stone—rejected by humans but chosen by God and precious to him— you also, like living stones, are being built into a spiritual house to be a holy priesthood, offering spiritual sacrifices acceptable to God through Jesus Christ. For in Scripture it says:

"See, I lay a stone in Zion,
a chosen and precious cornerstone,
and the one who trusts in him
will never be put to shame." . . .

But you are a chosen people, a royal priesthood, a holy nation, God's special possession, that you may declare the praises of him who called you out of darkness into his wonderful light. Once you were not a people, but now you are the people of God; once you had not received mercy, but now you have received mercy (1 Peter 2:4–6, 9–10).

How would you describe Peter's tone and attitude toward the church?

_____

_____

_____

_____

What can we learn from these verses about the structure and purpose of the church?

_____

_____

_____

_____

_____

LEADERSHIP AND MEMBERSHIP

The church is the physical representation of Christ on earth. What Jesus said, we are to say. What Jesus did, we are to do. What Jesus proclaimed, we are to proclaim. The world should be able to get a good idea about the nature and character of Christ by looking at His church. To carry out this mission requires a system of *leadership*—typically pastor-teachers, elders, and deacons. The Bible gives freedom as to how this leadership is organized but is specific about the spiritual qualities that are required for leaders. This is because these leaders must guide those who are *members* of the church—which occurs the moment a person becomes a Christian. Leaders are held to a high standard because they are responsible for guiding the members.

> Now the overseer is to be above reproach, faithful to his wife, temperate, self-controlled, respectable, hospitable, able to teach, not given to drunkenness, not violent but gentle, not quarrelsome, not a lover of money. He must manage his own family well and see that his children obey him, and he must do so in a manner worthy of full respect. (If anyone does not know how to manage his own family, how can he take care of God's church?) He must not be a recent convert, or he may become conceited and fall under the same judgment as the devil.

He must also have a good reputation with outsiders, so
that he will not fall into disgrace and into the devil's trap
(1 Timothy 3:2–7).

What are some of the qualifications that Paul says are needed for
a leader in the church?

_____

_____

_____

_____

How would you describe your role within your local church? What
about the church as a whole?

_____

_____

_____

_____

REVIEW

Look up the following passages and then indicate which of the
topics it supports regarding the doctrine of the church: *universal,
local, leadership,* or *membership.*

PASSAGES	TOPIC
1 Timothy 3:1–4; James 3:1–2:	
1 Corinthians 1:1–2; Matthew 18:20:	
Matthew 16:18; 1 Corinthians 12:27:	
Hebrews 10:24–25; Acts 2:42–44:	

DAY 30: THE DOCTRINE OF FUTURE THINGS

Wouldn't you love to know the future? Any of us would, which explains why there are entire industries dedicated to that field. Think of all the movies that have been made about the future. So-called "futurists" attempt to predict trends and patterns that will shape the world decades from now. And psychics make a living peddling vague promises about what might be around the corner for individuals. In light of this, it is interesting that the Bible opens a window into future events. What we can see through that window is hazy, and without specific details. Yet what we do see should encourage us to live our lives in obedience to Christ today.

RETURN AND JUDGMENT

Jesus was crucified, buried, and resurrected more than 2,000 years ago, but He promised that He would one day return to the earth. When this happens, He will not come as a carpenter's son from a humble village in Nazareth but as the Son of the King of the universe—and He will reveal His true sovereignty at that time over all of creation. Christians should look forward to this event, for the Bible reveals it will signal the final triumph over sin, evil, and death. Believers in Christ will be confirmed to eternity in heaven with Him. But those who refused to accept God's offer of salvation will be judged and confirmed to eternal separation from God in hell.

> "When the Son of Man comes in his glory, and all the angels with him, he will sit on his glorious throne. All the nations will be gathered before him, and he will separate the people one from another as a shepherd separates the sheep from the goats. He will put the sheep on his right and the goats on his left.

"Then the King will say to those on his right, 'Come, you who are blessed by my Father; take your inheritance, the kingdom prepared for you since the creation of the world. For I was hungry and you gave me something to eat, I was thirsty and you gave me something to drink, I was a stranger and you invited me in, I needed clothes and you clothed me, I was sick and you looked after me, I was in prison and you came to visit me.' . . .

"Then he will say to those on his left, 'Depart from me, you who are cursed, into the eternal fire prepared for the devil and his angels. For I was hungry and you gave me nothing to eat, I was thirsty and you gave me nothing to drink, I was a stranger and you did not invite me in, I needed clothes and you did not clothe me, I was sick and in prison and you did not look after me.' . . .

"Then they will go away to eternal punishment, but the righteous to eternal life" (Matthew 25:31–36, 41–43, 46).

What does Jesus say in this passage about His return? What does He say about judgment?

_____

_____

_____

_____

What are some ways that you are seeking to share the message of Christ with those who could be facing this judgment?

_____

_____

_____

UNIVERSE AND ETERNITY

The key truth we are told about the future is that God will be victorious. Jesus will reign in absolute righteousness, and the *universe* will be redeemed through the creation of a new heaven and earth that have not been corrupted by sin. Only goodness and beauty will exist. Believers in Christ will rule with Him in *eternity* as vice-regents in a world that glorifies God. We will govern angelic beings and kingdoms in the new earth. We will be beings of beauty and power who will participate in glorious celestial ceremonies. This glimpse of the future is largely the message communicated in the book of Revelation, the final book of the New Testament.

> Then I saw "a new heaven and a new earth," for the first heaven and the first earth had passed away, and there was no longer any sea. I saw the Holy City, the new Jerusalem, coming down out of heaven from God, prepared as a bride beautifully dressed for her husband. And I heard a loud voice from the throne saying, "Look! God's dwelling place is now among the people, and he will dwell with them. They will be his people, and God himself will be with them and be their God. 'He will wipe every tear from their eyes. There will be no more death' or mourning or crying or pain, for the old order of things has passed away."
>
> He who was seated on the throne said, "I am making everything new!" Then he said, "Write this down, for these words are trustworthy and true."
>
> He said to me: "It is done. I am the Alpha and the Omega, the Beginning and the End. To the thirsty I will give water without cost from the spring of the water of life. Those who are victorious will inherit all this, and

I will be their God and they will be my children. But
the cowardly, the unbelieving, the vile, the murderers,
the sexually immoral, those who practice magic arts,
the idolaters and all liars—they will be consigned to the
fiery lake of burning sulfur. This is the second death"
(Revelation 21:1-8).

What strikes you the most as you read the picture of the new heaven
and earth depicted in these verses? Why?

_____

_____

_____

_____

_____

How do the glimpses of heaven in the Scriptures influence your
desire to continue exploring and understanding the Bible?

_____

_____

_____

_____

_____

_____

REVIEW

Look up the following passages and then indicate which of the
topics it supports regarding the doctrine of future things: *return,
judgment, universe,* or *eternity.*

PASSAGES	TOPIC
2 Peter 3:12; Revelation 21:4:	
Matthew 16:27; Revelation 1:7:	
John 14:2–3; Revelation 22:5:	
2 Corinthians 5:10; Hebrews 9:27:	

Fill in the blanks from memory:

DOCTRINE	TOPIC
The Bible:	The Bible was _____ to humans by God. God _____ the words that were written. The Holy Spirit _____ the Bible so we can understand it. We must be diligent to _____ its teachings.
God:	God has _____ in the past and will _____ in the future. The Bible teaches _____ about His nature, one of which is that God is _____ over all creation. God exists in what we call the _____, consisting of the Father, Son, and Holy Spirit.
Christ:	Jesus was God-incarnate or _____, yet He was also fully _____ like us. After His death for our sin, He was _____ from the dead. He will one day _____ as a conquering king.
Holy Spirit:	The Holy Spirit is a _____ like God the Father and Jesus the Son and is fully _____ as well. He is instrumental in our _____, by which we receive God's forgiveness and experience eternal life. He also provides _____ for us to use to serve in the church.
Angels:	_____ are ministering spirits from God, while _____ are angels who _____ against God. _____is the highest angel who fell. God has given us _____ to guard against his attacks.
Man:	Man was _____ in God's image. We have both a _____ and _____ nature. We are _____ from other creatures, and we have an eternal _____ in either heaven or hell.

Sin:	We all have a _____ that leads us to sin against God. This began when sin entered the world at the _____, and since that time the world has been _____. Because of our internal nature, we continually struggle with sin and _____ against God.
Salvation:	The _____ of salvation is that it is a gift from God to those who _____. The _____ is that God extends forgiveness to us, exacted at a _____ through the sacrifice of Christ. Our salvation will be complete at the _____ of the death of our physical bodies.
Church:	The _____ church is the totality of all believers, while the _____ church is an assembly of believers in communities. Those in church _____ must possess certain spiritual _____. All Christians are _____ of the universal church.
Future Things:	Jesus will _____ to earth, at which time the world will be _____. The old _____ will be redeemed with a new _____ and a new _____. Believers will spend _____ ruling _____ Christ.

APPLY

Congratulations once again on completing this journey toward understanding the Bible! Your investments in engaging and studying God's Word will always produce a return because the Bible is a living, active Word that can never be exhausted. There is always more to learn! Check in with your partner one last time this week to review what you studied. Use the following questions to help cement the main concepts in your minds.

- **Doctrine of Man:** The Bible teaches we are more than just our physical bodies—but that doesn't mean our bodies are unimportant. Discuss with your partner one practical step you can take this week to better care for and appreciate the body you have received from your loving heavenly Father.

- **Doctrine of Sin:** If *sin* is a word that makes people uncomfortable, then so is *confession*. Discuss with your partner the importance of confessing sins. If you feel comfortable, share one area in which you struggle.

- **Doctrine of Salvation:** Many Christians today live as if doing good deeds and avoiding sin is the basis of their connection with God. Test this in your own lives by considering whether you have a tendency to "make deals" with God. Do you feel as if God loves you less when you make mistakes? Do you judge others by their mistakes or failures rather than by the grace of God?

- **Doctrine of the Church:** The church is the gathering of all who follow Christ in every corner of the world—past, present, and future. However, buildings are still an important part of the church experience. Join with your partner to walk your church grounds. Pick up any trash you see, get rid of weeds, and take any steps you can take to show your appreciation for your local church.

- **Doctrine of Future Things:** Discuss your thoughts related to the prophecies you have read concerning the return of Christ. What uncertainties do you have? What hope do you have? What are your general feelings when you consider the end of life on this earth as you know it?

MOVING FORWARD

In the weeks ahead, you may want to review sections 4–6 in *30 Days to Understanding the Bible,* which provides a nano summary of the Bible, tips for mastering the Bible so well it masters you, a teaching plan, and eight bonus chapters. Consider what Bible study, group ministry, or service area God would have you participate in next. Whatever you choose, make a commitment to continue learning about the Bible and understanding its content.

ANSWERS TO REVIEW QUESTIONS

SESSION 1: AN OVERVIEW OF THE BIBLE

Day 1: 39, 27, 66; Hebrew; historical, poetical, prophetical

Day 2: (1) Mediterranean Sea, (2) Sea of Galilee, (3) Jordan River, (4) Dead Sea, (5) Nile River, (6) Tigris River, (7) Euphrates River, (8) Persian Gulf, (A) Garden of Eden, (B) Canaan/Israel, (C) Jerusalem, (D) Egypt, (E) Assyria, (F) Babylonia, (G) Persia.

Day 3: Old Testament: (1) Creation Era, (2) Patriarch Era, (3) Exodus Era, (4) Conquest Era, (5) Judges Era, (6) Kingdom Era, (7) Exile Era, (8) Return Era, (9) Silence Era; New Testament: (1) Gospel Era, (2) Church Era, (3) Missions Era.

Day 4: (Day 1) light and darkness, (Day 2) waters and sky, (Day 3) land and vegetation, (Day 4) sun and moon, (Day 5) sea creatures and birds, (Day 6) land animals and humans, (After Creation) the fall / sin entered the world.

Day 5: 4, 3, 1, 2; sinned, fall, plan.

SESSION 2: THE EARLY HISTORY OF ISRAEL

Day 6: 3, 4, 1, 2

Day 7: 4, 1, 2, 3

Day 8: 2, 4, 1, 3

Day 9: 2, 3, 4, 1

Day 10: *Exercise 1:* 2, 4, 1, 3; *Exercise 2:* sinned, fall, plan; called, nation; freed, Egypt; conquest, Promised Land; judges, lead; United, Israel, Judah

SESSION 3: THE LATER HISTORY OF ISRAEL

Day 11: 3, 4, 2, 1

Day 12: 3, 2, 1, 4

Day 13: 2, 4, 1, 3

Day 14: 2, 4, 5, 1, 3

Day 15: *Exercise 1:* 4, 3, 1, 2; *Exercise 2:* sinned, fall, plan; called, nation; freed, Egypt; conquest, Promised Land; judges, lead; United, Israel, Judah; conquest, captivity; Jerusalem, walls, law; Maccabaeans, Zealots, Pharisees, Sadducees

SESSION 4: THE HISTORY OF THE CHURCH

Day 16: *Geography of the Gospels:* (1) Mediterranean Sea, (2) Sea of Galilee, (3) Jordan River, (4) Dead Sea, (A) Galilee, (B) Samaria, (C) Judea, (D) Perea, (E) Nazareth, (F) Capernaum, (G) Jerusalem, (H) Bethlehem; *Geography of Acts:* (1) Mediterranean Sea, (2) Sea of Galilee, (3) Jordan River, (4) Dead Sea, (A) Galatia, (B) Greece, (C) Asia, (D) Italy, (E) Jerusalem, (F) Damascus, (G) Caesarea, (H) Antioch, (I) Rome

Day 17: 3, 1, 4, 2

Day 18: 3, 1, 4, 2

Day 19: 2, 4, 3, 1

Day 20: *Exercise 1:* 4, 2, 1, 3; *Exercise 2:* sinned, fall, plan; called, nation; freed, Egypt; conquest, Promised Land; judges, lead; United, Israel, Judah; conquest, captivity; Jerusalem, walls, law; Maccabaeans, Zealots, Pharisees, Sadducees; teaching, miracles, reject, resurrection; church, persecution; missionary, Gentiles

SESSION 5: THE BIBLE, GOD, CHRIST, THE HOLY SPIRIT, AND ANGELS

Day 21: illumination, revelation, interpretation, inspiration

Day 22: Trinity, divine attributes, sovereignty, existence, personal attributes

Day 23: resurrection, humanity, return, deity

Day 24: gifts, deity, salvation, personality

Day 25: *Exercise 1:* angels, Satan, defenses, demons; *Exercise 2:* revealed, inspired, illuminates, interpret; existed, exist, attributes, sovereign, Trinity; divine, human, resurrected, return; person, divine, salvation, gifts; angels, demons, rebelled, Satan, defenses

SESSION 6: MAN, SIN, SALVATION, THE CHURCH, AND FUTURE THINGS

Day 26: distinctiveness, destiny, origin, nature

Day 27: nature, rebellion, corruption, fall

Day 28: cost, timing, basis, result

Day 29: leadership, local, universal, membership

Day 30: *Exercise 1:* universe, return, eternity, judgment; *Exercise 2:* revealed, inspired, illuminates, interpret; existed, exist, attributes, sovereign, Trinity; divine, human, resurrected, return; person, divine, salvation, gifts; angels, demons, rebelled, Satan, defenses; created, spiritual, physical, distinct, destiny; nature, fall, corrupt, rebellion; basis, believe, result, cost, time; universal, local, leadership, qualifications, members; return, judged, universe, heaven, earth, eternity

LEADER'S GUIDE

Thank you for your willingness to lead your group through this study! What you have chosen to do is valuable and will make a great difference in the lives of others. The rewards of being a leader are different from those of participating, and we hope that as you lead you will find your own walk with Jesus deepened by this experience.

30 Days to Understanding the Bible is a six-session study built around video content and small-group interaction. As the group leader, just think of yourself as the host of a dinner party. Your job is to take care of your guests by managing all the behind-the-scenes details so that when everyone arrives, they can just enjoy time together.

As the group leader, your role is not to answer all the questions or reteach the content—the video, book, and study guide will do most of that work. Your job is to guide the experience and cultivate your small group into a kind of teaching community. This will make it a place for members to process, question, and reflect—not receive more instruction.

Before your first meeting, make sure everyone in the group gets a copy of the study guide. This will keep everyone on the same page and help the process run more smoothly. If some group members are unable to purchase the guide, arrange it so that people can share the resource with other group members. Giving everyone access to all the material will position this study to be as rewarding an experience as possible. Everyone should feel free to write in his or her study guide and bring it to group every week.

SETTING UP THE GROUP

You will need to determine with your group how long you want to meet each week so you can plan your time accordingly. Generally, most groups like to meet for either ninety minutes or two hours, so you could use one of the following schedules:

SECTION	90 MINUTES	120 MINUTES
WELCOME (members arrive and get settled)	10 minutes	15 minutes
SHARE (discuss one or more of the opening questions for the session)	15 minutes	15 minutes
WATCH (watch the teaching material together and take notes)	20 minutes	20 minutes
DISCUSS (discuss the Bible study questions you selected ahead of time)	30 minutes	55 minutes
APPLY (group partners meet together to reflect on the topic of the session)	15 minutes	15 minutes

As the group leader, you will want to create an environment that encourages sharing and learning. A church sanctuary or formal classroom may not be as ideal as a living room, because those locations can feel formal and less intimate. No matter what setting you choose, provide enough comfortable seating for everyone, and, if possible, arrange the seats in a semicircle so everyone can see the video easily. This will make transition between the video and group conversation more efficient and natural.

Try to get to the meeting site early so you can greet participants as they arrive. Simple refreshments create a welcoming atmosphere and can be a wonderful addition to a group study evening. Try to take food and pet allergies into account to make your guests as comfortable as possible. You may also want to consider offering childcare to couples with children who want to attend. Finally, be sure your media technology is working properly. Managing these details up front will make the rest of your group experience flow smoothly and provide a welcoming space to engage the content of *30 Days to Understanding the Bible*.

STARTING THE GROUP TIME

Once everyone has arrived, it's time to begin the group. Here are some simple tips to make your group time healthy, enjoyable, and effective.

First, begin the meeting with a short prayer and remind the group members to put their phones on silent. This is a way to make sure you can all be present with one another and with God. Next, give each person a few minutes to respond to the questions in the "Share" sections. This won't require as much time in session one, but beginning in session two, people will need more time to share their insights from their personal studies. Usually, you won't answer the discussion questions yourself, but you should go first with the "Share" questions, answering briefly and with a reasonable amount of transparency.

At the end of session one, invite the group members to complete the between-sessions personal studies for that week. Explain that you will be providing some time before the video teaching next week for anyone to share insights. Let them know sharing is optional.

LEADING THE DISCUSSION TIME

Now that the group is engaged, it's time to watch the video and respond with some directed small-group discussion. Encourage all the group members to participate in the discussion, but make sure they know they don't have to do so. As the discussion progresses, you may want to follow up with comments such as, "Tell me more about that," or, "Why did you answer that way?" This will allow the group participants to deepen their reflections and invite meaningful sharing in a nonthreatening way.

Note that you have been given multiple questions to use in each session, and you do not have to use them all or even follow them in order. Feel free to pick and choose questions based on either the needs of your group or how the conversation is flowing. Also, don't be afraid of silence. Offering a question and allowing up to thirty seconds of silence is okay. It allows people space to think about how they want to respond and also gives them time to do so.

As group leader, you are the boundary keeper for your group. Do not let anyone (yourself included) dominate the group time. Keep an eye out for group members who might be tempted to "attack" folks they disagree with or try to "fix" those having struggles. These kinds of behaviors can derail a group's momentum, so they need to be steered in a different direction. Model active listening and encourage everyone in your group to do the same. This will make your group time a safe space and create a positive community.

The group discussion leads to a closing time of application. Encourage the participants to take a few moments to meet with the partner they have selected and review what they've learned during the session. This will help them cement the big ideas in their minds as you close the session.

Thank you again for taking the time to lead your group. You are making a difference in the lives of others and having an impact on the kingdom of God!

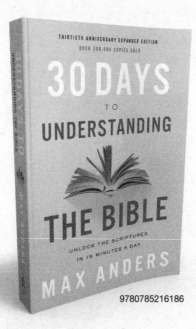